MW01098462

Carving Trophy Deer & Elk

by Todd A. Swaim

Fox Chapel Publishing Co., Inc.
1970 Broad Street
East Petersburg, PA 17520

Copyright © 1998 Fox Chapel Publishing Company Inc.

Carving Trophy Deer & Elk is a brand new work first published in 1998 by Fox Chapel Publishing Company, Inc. The patterns contained herein are copyrighted by the author. Artists may make any number of projects based on these patterns. The patterns themselves, however, are not to be photocopied for resale or distribution under any circumstances. Any such copying is a violation of copyright laws.

Publisher: Alan Giagnocavo
Project Editor: Ayleen Stellhorn
Desktop Specialist: Robert Altland, Altland Design

ISBN# 1–56523–089–2

To order your copy of this book,
please send check or money order
for $19.95 plus $2.50 shipping to:
Fox Books Orders
1970 Broad Street
East Petersburg, PA 17520

Manufactured in China

A friendly tip for woodcarvers...

We would like to pass along information on the best deal we have ever seen for woodcarvers.

The National Wood Carvers Association is a non-profit organization dedicated to the art of woodcarving. Members receive six issues of "Chip Chats," a colorful magazine full of techniques, show happenings, photographs of masterworks and more.

We highly recommend that every carver from beginner to professional join—you won't be disappointed.

Membership is only $11.00 per year ($14 outside USA)
National Wood Carvers Association
7424 Miami Ave.
Cincinnati, OH 45243

Twelve years ago when I first began carving, I had no idea I would be interested in creating a carving book, not to mention, the advanced skills and quality of work it would take to make such a book. At that time, when I first began carving, my only goal was to be able to carve a few "neat" pieces to decorate my home. Now, through twelve years of study, research and experience, my new set of goals includes being able to teach others some of the techniques that I have learned.

About a year ago I began teaching one-on-one woodcarving classes in my home studio. Through these classes I have found it to be very important to combine beginning, intermediate and advanced techniques to be suitable for each student's particular skills. Likewise, an advanced carver may pick up on a simple technique that could have been overlooked in one of his or her beginner carving classes.

I hope to explain everything from beginner to advanced techniques in as much detail as possible, so as not to leave any unanswered questions.   —*Todd A. Swaim*

"EVERY HUNTERS DREAM"
WHITETAIL BUCK
Handcarved by Todd Swaim.

WHITE TAIL DEER BY TODD A. SWAIM

CLOSE-UPS OF WHITE TAIL DEER

MULE DEER BY TODD A. SWAIM

CLOSE-UPS OF MULE DEER BY TODD A. SWAIM

BULL ELK by Todd A. Swaim

CLOSE-UPS OF BULL ELK BY TODD A. SWAIM

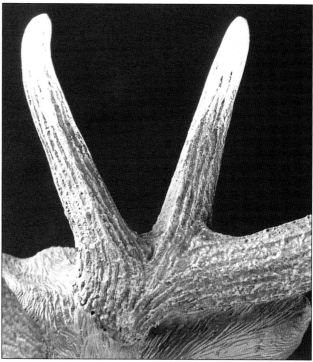

CLOSE-UPS OF BULL ELK BY TODD A. SWAIM

Chapter One

Patterns, Reference and Wood Selection

Patterns! Patterns! Patterns! Let me start by saying that creating a pattern is one of the most important steps in carving. It has been my experience that a carving is only as good as its pattern. You can take a bad pattern and make an "OK" woodcarving, but it takes a good pattern to make a great carving. So with this in mind, you must spend whatever time it takes to make a good quality, anatomically correct pattern.

When I begin to make a pattern I gather as many photos as I can of the subject I am going to carve. Ideally, these photos show as many angles as possible. When I transfer a photo of an animal to a piece of paper, I make sure that the photo I am using is as close as possible to a broadside view. I then use an opaque projector to project the animal's image on paper to the size that I want the pattern to be. I mark down as much detail as possible, including eyes, antler bases, nose, ears and any muscle lines. At this point you are ready to cut out the pattern and transfer it to a block of wood. You'll find patterns for the projects in this book in Appendix A.

If you are using basswood, it is very important to lay out your pattern in a manner that allows the grain of wood to work to your advantage. What I mean by this is that if you are carving a bull elk, you would need to lay the pattern on the wood so that the grain will run parallel to the main beams of the antlers. This position will give the antlers maximum strength. If you use tupelo, I have found that it is not

Photo 1.1 *Large blocks of tupelo wood are easy to obtain. The large size makes them perfect for big game trophy carving.*

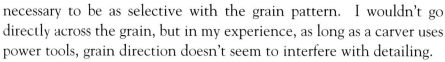

necessary to be as selective with the grain pattern. I wouldn't go directly across the grain, but in my experience, as long as a carver uses power tools, grain direction doesn't seem to interfere with detailing.

A very large number of carvers use basswood, but I prefer tupelo. There are several very important reasons why I choose tupelo over basswood for carving big game animals. First, large pieces of tupelo are easier to obtain. I carve mostly big game animals that have a wide antler spread. Large game birds and birds of prey require larger pieces of wood. If I used basswood, I would have to bond several pieces together to achieve the size that I need. I deal with a supplier who supplies me with pieces of tupelo that are as large as six feet in length and twelve inches square. Second, I prefer tupelo because of its strength and flexibility. When carving big game animals I encounter many fragile parts, such as antlers, horns, hooves, ears and tails. Third, tupelo is very porous, which enables me to soak the fragile parts in super glue to enhance the strength ten-fold. And fourth, tupelo's grain is much finer than basswood, which allows me to texture hair much easier.

Before you begin cutting into your block of wood it is very important to have all your reference materials that you are using for your project close at hand. In this case, deer and elk reference materials. When I use the term reference material, I am referring to anything that could possibly help you understand your subject. Pictures, skulls, antlers, fur samples and deer or elk mounts are perfect examples. I do almost all of my carvings from photos or wildlife books. There are many excellent wildlife books out there on the market today that can be excellent sources of reference material. Your local public library and the closest game and fish department may also be willing to help you with reference photos

At this point I would like to point out that it is important not to restrict yourself by working from only one or two photos. Not all deer and elk are the same. For example, you may have two bull elk with 6 x 6 antlers that are approximately the same age, but one may have a head or skull that measures 18 inches long and 10 inches wide while the skull of the other might measure 16 inches long and 9 inches wide. The main reason I point this out is that I have carving students who get concerned over the fact that their deer or elk doesn't have the same measurements as one that I have done. It is the same with deer and elk antlers. Each animal has its own unique shape and size. The reference photos on the following pages will give you a good starting point for comparison.

Photo 1.2 *White tail buck laying down.*

Photo 1.3 *Notice the large shoulder bone structure and muscle in this side view of a white tail mount.*

Photo 1.4 *A front view of a white tail buck shows the wide rutting neck.*

Photo 1.5 *A close-up shows how the eyes of this white tail buck are set slightly forward. This photo also shows excellent nose features.*

Photo 1.6 *A close-up of a white tail's ear shows the detail of this area.*

Photo 1.7 *A large mule deer buck is shown in this photo.*

Photo 1.8 *Take notice of the large ears on the young mule deer bucks in this photo. This is a distinctive feature among mule deer.*

Photo 1.9 *A front view of a mule deer buck shows how the lower chest protrudes the body and shoulders.*

Photo 1.10 *The nose and mouth can be easily studied in this side view.*

Photo 1.11 *A mule deer's nose is very similar to a white tail's nose.*

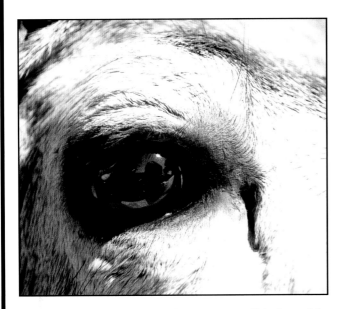

Photo 1.12 *Notice the scent gland groove coming off the front of the eye in this close-up of a deer's eye.*

Photo 1.13 *This is an abnormally small ear for a mule deer, but yet still larger than a white tail's ear.*

Photo 1.14 *A large bull elk.*

Photo 1.15 *Notice how the head tips back when a bull elk bugles.*

Photo 1.16 *A close up of a bull elk's mouth shows teeth, lips, nose and tongue.*

Photo 1.17 *Summer coats show animal muscle and bone features better.*

Chapter Two
Cutting Out and Roughing Down

Now that you have your pattern transferred onto a block of wood, you are ready to cut it out on a band saw. I am very fortunate to own a band saw that will cut a whopping 12 3/4 inches. I rarely cut a piece of wood of this size because accuracy is sacrificed. When cutting something as small as the tips of antlers on a very thick block, the blade sometimes tends to pull with the harder grain of wood. The result may very well be an antler that is 1/2 inch on the top of the block and 1/4 inch on the bottom side. When this happens, the piece is already ruined. So, because of this, I usually cut a block no more than six inches thick.

All of the patterns included in Appendix A could be cut from a block of wood that is 4 inches thick for the deer and 6 3/4 inches for the elk. If you only have access to a band saw that will cut a three-inch piece of wood, I have included a splicing technique for making the antlers wide enough. Using the same splicing technique, you can also give the animal bust movement.

Throughout this book, you'll find photographs and instructions specific to carving a white tail deer bust. Interspersed with these photographs are pictures specific to carving a bull elk bust. The steps for carving a bull elk and mule deer are similar to those for carving a white tail deer, so I did not go into those in detail. Simply follow the instructions for the white tail deer but use the pattern for the animal of your choice.

If you only have the means to cut a block of wood three inches or less, begin by cutting the pattern from a three-inch block. I have shown this with the white tail deer in Photo 2.2. Then copy the same pattern of the antlers on another three-inch block and cut the antlers out. Run the antlers on end through the band saw and divide them directly down the center so you have two antlers as shown in Photo 2.3. This will give you the desired antler thickness with some extra, depending on how wide you choose to make your antlers. If you are carving a bust with the head straight forward, you would now bond the two antlers onto the deer body as shown in Photo 2.4. Epoxy is better than wood glue because you don't need a tight fit like you would get with wood glue. If you have a reasonably straight cut on your wood you can put the pieces together without clamping them and without a lot of wood preparation. Epoxy has proven to be very reliable for me.

If you choose to give the bust more movement, do not bond the antlers to the body until you have cut the neck on the bust. Gluing the antlers causes them to be in the way when you cut the neck on the band saw. To give the bust movement, begin by cutting directly through the center of the neck. Then cut an angled slice off of the back half of the bust as shown in Photo 2.6. The degree of the angle doesn't make a difference, it will only make the neck turn more or less. On this pattern, I used a measurement of one inch on the wide side of the angle. This is about right for the size of this bust. Flip over the same angled slice that you just cut out of the center of the bust as shown in Photo 2.7. Because of the shape of the neck, the slice will not be tall enough to fill the gap. The narrow end of the angle will be cut out of the center of the neck on the opposite side, so when you flip the angled cut block over it will not be tall enough. For this, cut a slice of wood with the same angle only taller. Refer to Photo 2.8. Discard the smaller angle of wood. You will only need the taller slice. Now, you are ready to bond the three pieces of wood back together, making sure that the front half of the bust is centered with the back half. The slice of wood that goes in the center must be even with the back and front halves, as shown in Photo 2.9. It is very important that you make these pieces even because this will keep the neck the same length as it was before you cut it. At this point, you can bond the two antler pieces that you cut out earlier in this chapter to the bust as shown in Photo 2.10.

You are now ready to rough your piece down. Every wood carver has his or her own way of taking the bulk of the wood off in a hurry. I am no exception. I prefer to use a four inch grinder with a chain saw blade disc. This is a very dangerous piece of equipment, but like any other power tool you need to have a set of safety rules to go by. This grinder will peel off a one inch layer of wood with one pass or will shave off the finest amount of wood and leave the wood very smooth.

After I have put a center line all the way around the deer or elk bust as demonstrated in Photo 2.11, I mark the outside dimensions on all the different sections of the bust, including the antlers, as shown in Photos 2.12 and 2.13. This way I can trim off some of the bulk with the band saw. It will also give me a guide to follow so that I don't trim off too much with the chain saw disc. I then start by clamping the block of wood to a sturdy bench and begin shaving off all the squared edges, as shown in Photos 2.15 and 2.16. You will need to make sure to keep your pattern close by so you can continually make measurements and markings for the correct placement of the ears, eye sockets, and shoulders. See Photos 2.17, 2.18 and 2.19. Be careful! It is very easy to take too much off. I always leave the wood around the ear area completely intact until almost last. Refer to Photo 2.20. After I've taken as much wood off as I possibly can with the four-inch grinder, I then move on to a small sanding drum and begin smoothing up all cut marks and edges made by the grinder. Once I have removed all the rough edges, I start removing the excess wood from areas that the big four-inch grinder couldn't reach. When you take the wood out between the antlers you will loose the rest of your center line that gave you your reference points to go by to keep the antlers even. Make sure you have good pencil marks on the part of the antler where the points will be before you remove the center line between the antlers. See Photos 2.21 and 2.22.

On a deer bust remember that you need to leave a section of wood between the antlers, as shown in Photo 2.23. This is where the brow points will be. When I think things are finally beginning to take shape, I start drawing on all the muscles, eye sockets and ear positions as I go. I continue to grind these areas down a little at a time to form a well-rounded neck and head. You may have to redraw the lines for muscles, eyes and ears many times until you get the desired thickness and shape you want.

Photo 2.1 *Draw the white tail deer pattern on a block of wood.*

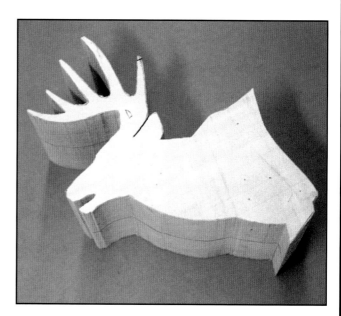

Photo 2.2 *Cut out the bust on a bandsaw.*

Photo 2.3 *This photo shows both antler extensions before bonding to the deer bust.*

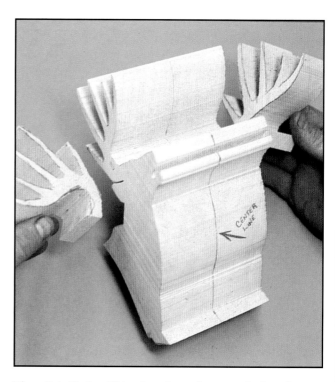

Photo 2.4 *Fit the additional wooden antlers to get the desired thickness.*

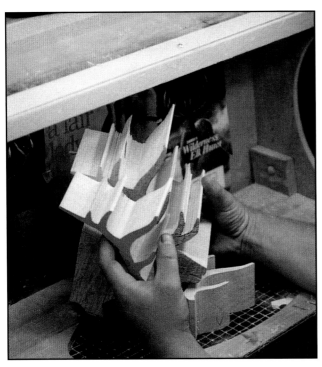

Photo 2.5 *If you are working on an elk bust, now fit the additional wooden antlers onto the bust to get the desired antler spread.*

Photo 2.6 *Cut an angled slice to give the white tail's neck curvature.*

Photo 2.7 *This photo shows the angled cut block flipped over.*

Photo 2.8 *Here is a second cut angled block next to one with the same angle, only taller.*

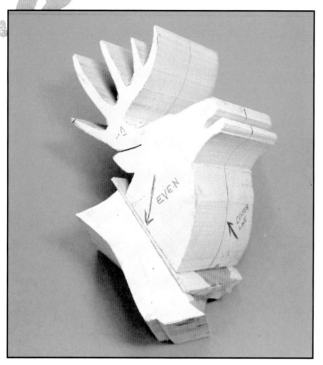

Photo 2.9 *This photo shows all three pieces bonded back together to make one.*

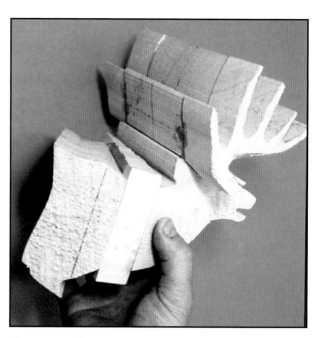

Photo 2.10 *The two antler blocks of wood now have been added.*

Photo 2.11 *If you're working on an elk bust, mark the center line on the bust at this time.*

Photo 2.12 and 2.13 *Mark the outside maximum measurement of a deer bust.*

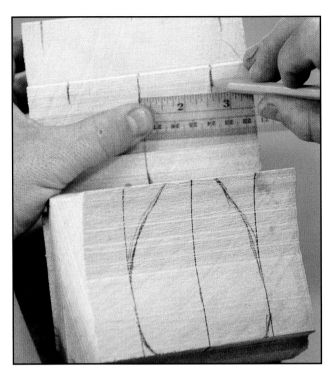

Photo 2.13

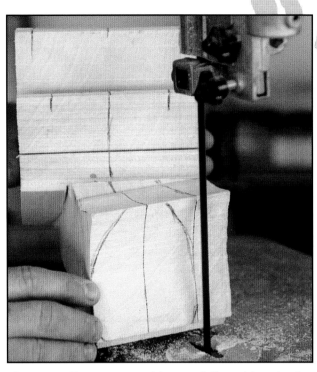

Photo 2.14 *Trim away some of the excess bulk wood from the white tail deer bust.*

Photo 2.15 *Rough the deer bust with a four-inch grinder.*

Photo 2.16 *Rough the elk bust. I cut all the excess wood from in between the antlers with the four-inch grinder or a ¹/2″ coarse sanding drum.*

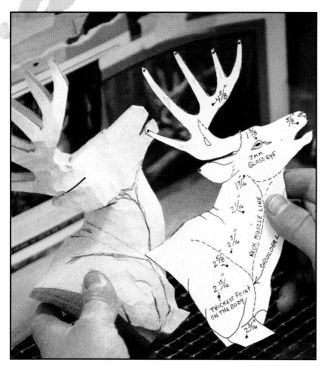

Photo 2.17 *Mark the shoulder and neck muscle lines on the deer bust.*

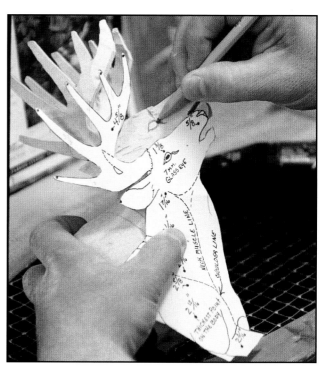

Photo 2.18 *Use the pattern to measure the location of eye.*

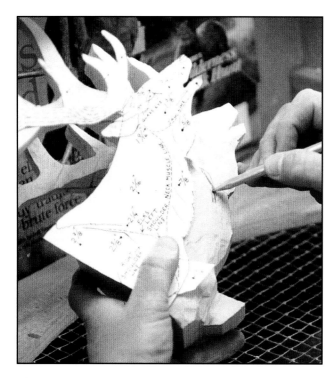

Photo 2.19 *If you're working on an elk bust, mark neck muscle lines on the bust at this time.*

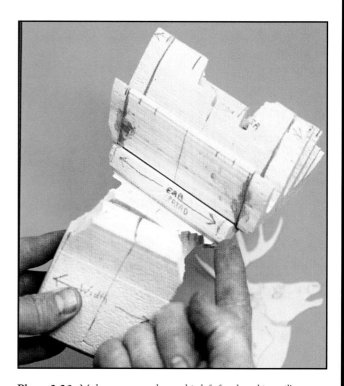

Photo 2.20 *Make sure enough wood is left for the white tail's ears.*

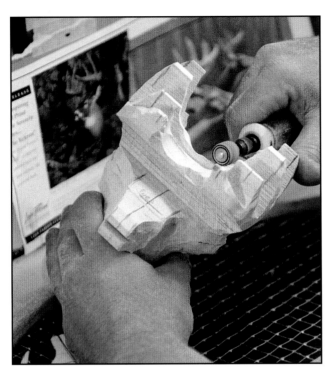

Photo 2.21 *Remove excess wood from between the antlers with a ¹/₂" sanding drum. Notice the antler point markings. These markings must always stay on the bust until the antlers are completely shaped.*

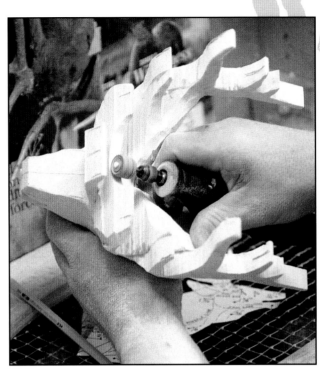

Photo 2.22 *If you're working on a bull elk, cut out the interior sections of the elk's antlers.*

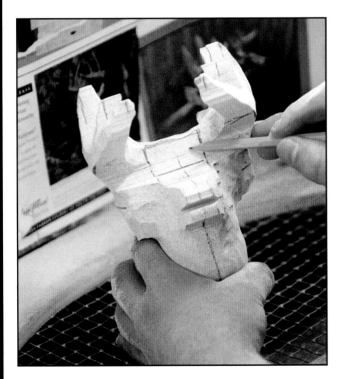

Photo 2.23 *This photo shows the area where the brow points will be located on the deer bust.*

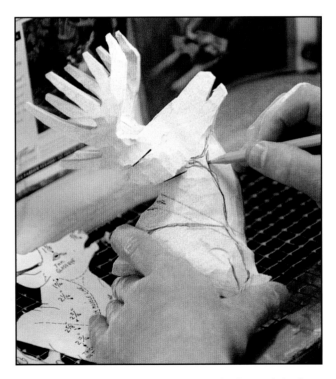

Photo 2.24 *After you have smoothed the rough edges made by the four inch grinder, draw the neck and shoulder lines again.*

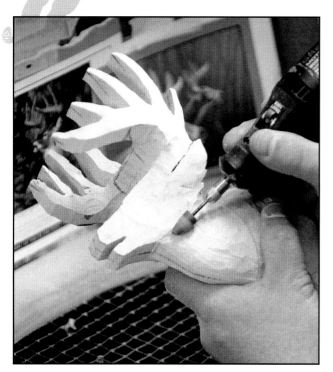

Photo 2.25 *Round and refine the neck muscles on the deer bust with a ³/8″ cone-shaped ruby carver bit.*

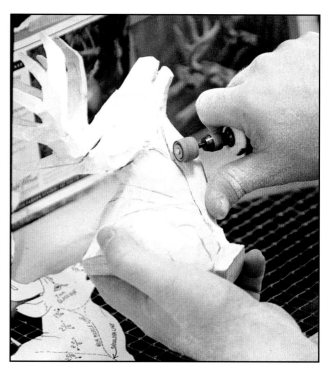

Photo 2.26 *If you need to remove more wood, first redraw the neck and shoulder lines then carve down a little more.*

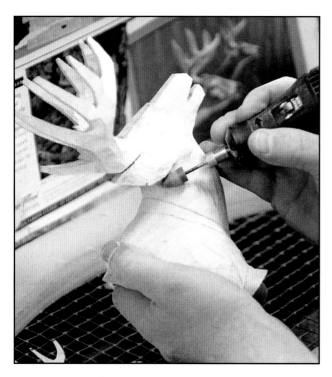

Photo 2.27 *Grind excess wood from around the deer's ears using a cone shaped burr.*

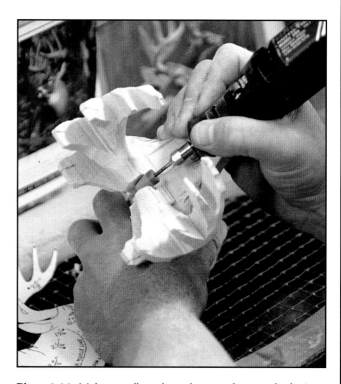

Photo 2.28 *Make a small cut down the center between the deer's antlers. Be careful not to cut too deep or you will cut into the top of the deer's head.*

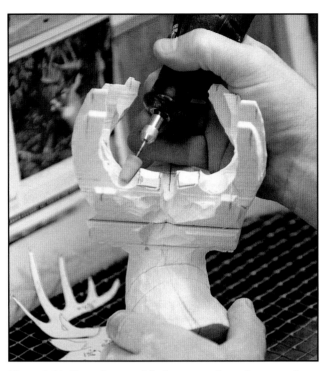

Photo 2.29 *Form the tops of the brow points by making a small cut on the outer sides of the brow points. The deer bust is now ready for the refinement techniques covered in Chapter 3.*

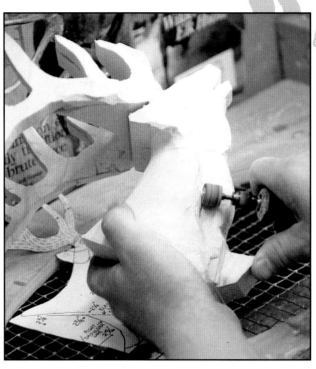

Photo 2.30 *To complete the roughing out of the bull elk bust, begin by refining the elk's neck muscle.*

Photo 2.31 *On this particular elk bust, with the left leg forward and the right one back, cut off the right leg from the center line out as indicated in the photo.*

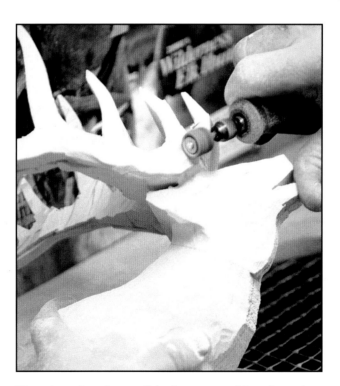

Photo 2.32 *Start shaving off the sharp corners of the antler on the elk.*

Photo 2.33 *Take the excess off around the elk's ears.*

Photo 2.34 *Shape the shoulder line on the right shoulder.*

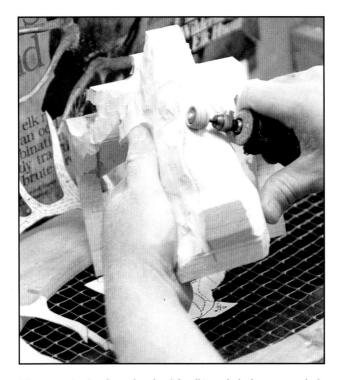

Photo 2.35 *On the underside of the elk's neck the hair is very thick and wavy. Draw a wavy line along the center line from the elk's chin to the elk's chest. Then grind up to the wavy line on each side. This will give your elk's head a little grace and movement.*

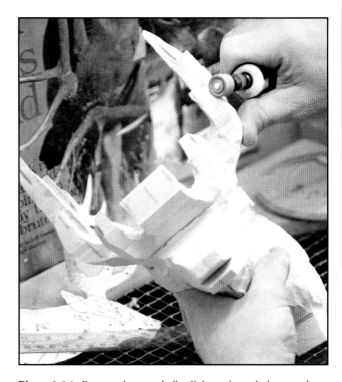

Photo 2.36 *Remove the extra bulk off the antlers a little on each side, one at a time. Never remove all the excess wood from one side before going to the next side. This could result in uneven antlers.*

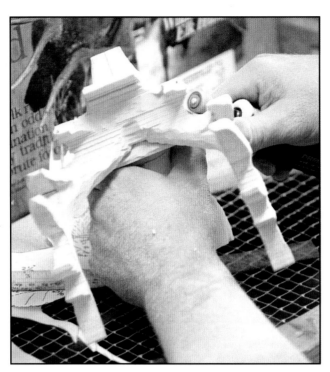

Photo 2.37 *Hint: If you remove a little off of the third point on one side, then remove the same amount on the third point on the other side. Do not skip around. Have some sort of order when taking off the bulk on the antlers.*

Photo 2.38 *Once you have carved the antlers to the desired thickness, begin shaping each point.*

Photo 2.39 *Then cut a small gap between the front brow points with a 1/4" pointed diamond bit. Make sure you are right over the center line on top of the elk's forehead.*

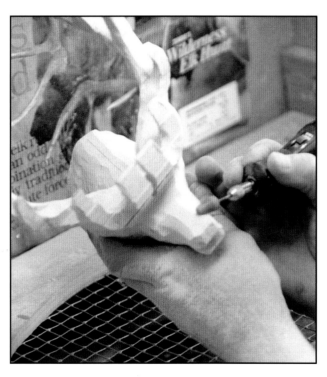

Photo 2.40 *Round the edges on the bull elk's head. The bull elk is now ready for the refining stage.*

Chapter Three

Refining the Face, Antlers, Eyes and Ears

To begin refining you just pick up where you left off from Chapter 2. I usually use a small, medium to fine grit, grinding bit. I prefer diamond bits to grinding stones because they tend not to get filled with wood particles. When diamond bits get filled with wood particles they can be easily cleaned out by using a torch to burn them out. There is no set order that I use when it comes to putting in the eyes or working on the nose or mouth. Just make sure that you have the desired thickness that you need in the area that you are working on.

To pick up where we left off in Chapter 2, I begin by taking the last remaining bulk off of the antlers and ears, as shown in Photo 3.1.

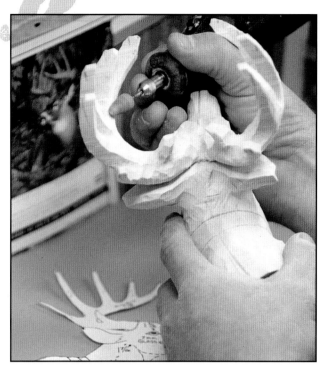

Photo 3.1 *Remove the last bit of bulk from the deer antlers with a 3" ruby carver burr.*

Photo 3.2 *Round some of the edges of the antler points.*

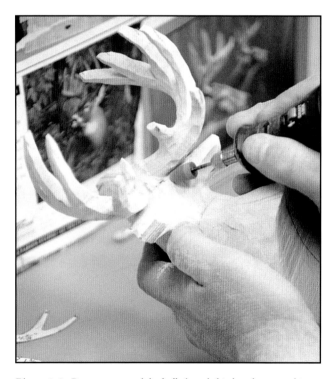

Photo 3.3 *Remove some of the bulk from behind each ear, making sure to leave the ear plenty thick until you have shaped the front side of the deer's ear.*

Photo 3.4 *This photo shows the carved down sections of the brow point areas.*

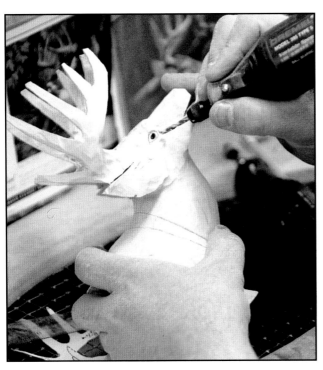

Photo 3.5 *Use the pattern to measure again where the eye hole will be. I like to do this before I carve the front of the ears because where the front of the ear begins and ends depends solely on the location of the eye. I mark a permanent eye hole where the eye should be by drilling a hole straight in the deer's head about half way in to the other side with a ¹/8″ drill bit.*

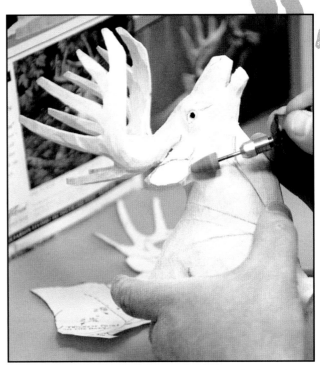

Photo 3.6 *Now that the eye hole is marked, shape the front of the deer's ears.*

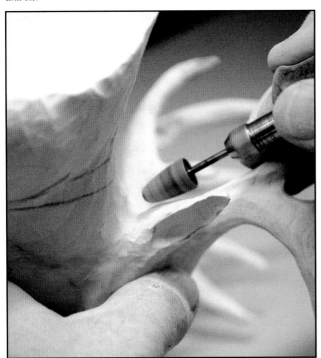

Photo 3.7 *Once the front of the deer's ears are shaped the way you like them, finish thinning down the back of the ear to the desired thickness.*

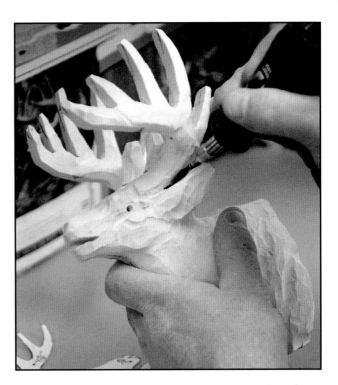

Photo 3.8 *Finish the ear by cutting the groove between the antler and top of the ear with a ¹/4″ pointed diamond burr.*

Photo 3.9 *I use a small round ball burr and open the eye hole around the drilled hole to about 7–8 mm. in diameter. This is the size of a glass eye that I will be using for this deer.*

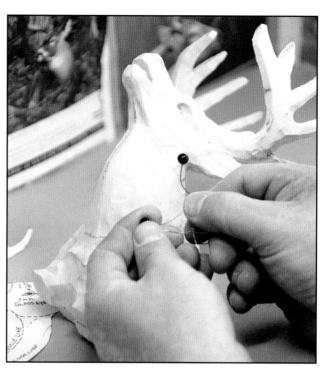

Photo 3.10 *Break the glass eyes off the wire (if they come on a wire) and check to make sure they fit in the hole you have just created.*

Photo 3.11 *Fill the eye holes about half way with a good quality wood filler.*

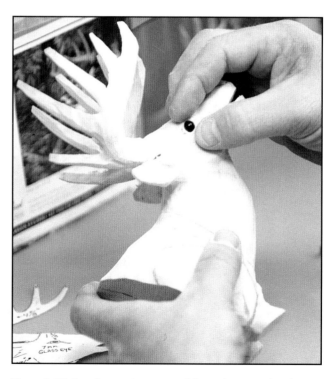

Photo 3.12 *Lay the eyes in very carefully, making sure that they are straight.*

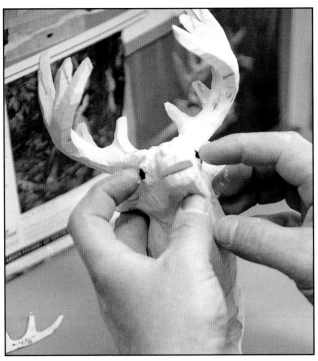

Photo 3.13 *Hold the deer's head so that it is looking straight at you and push evenly on both sides at the same time. You should also look down from the top view to make sure that the eyes are even from the top angle. At this point, allow the eyes to dry for at least 24 hours.*

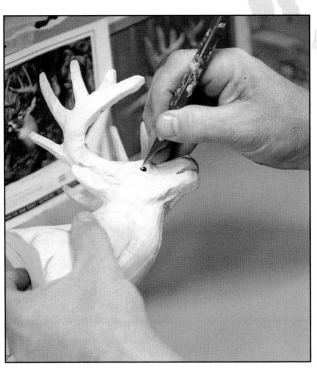

Photo 3.14 *Once the filler has dried, use an exacto-knife to clean all of the excess fill off the face of the glass eye.*

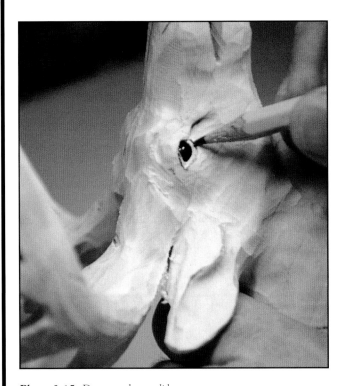

Photo 3.15 *Draw on the eye lids.*

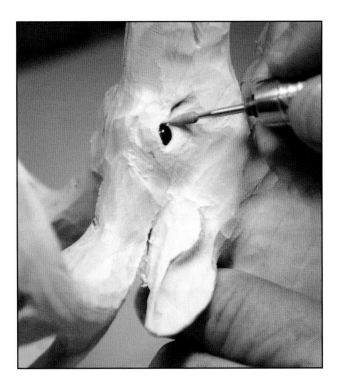

Photo 3.16 *Use a very small, fine cone-shaped diamond bit to carve the eye lid. When doing this I leave the portion between the pencil line and glass eye protruding slightly. At this time I also cut a small groove in front of the eye. This is one of the deer's many scent glands. I make this cut approximately 1/16 of an inch deep and slightly upward.*

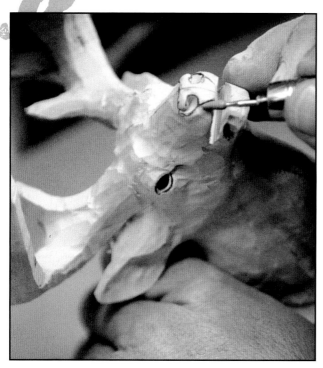

Photo 3.17 *Use the same small cone-shaped bit to cut the deer's nostrils. I usually draw the deer's nose on first. This gives me a guide to go on so that both sides end up even.*

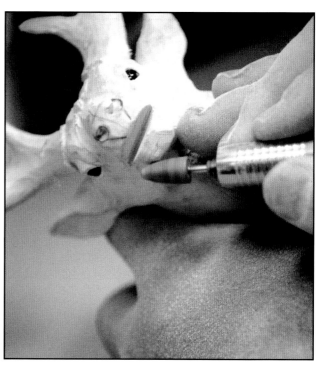

Photo 3.18 *Once you have the nose done, trim down the bottom jaw so that it is slightly narrower than the upper jaw. In true life, the bottom jaw of a deer or elk fits up into the upper jaw.*

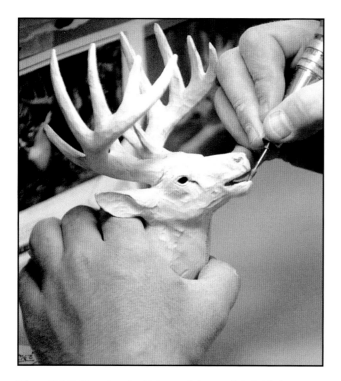

Photo 3.19 *Now that the thickness of the mouth is finished, carve the inside of the mouth. On a bust of this size it is very hard to demonstrate what the inside of a deer's or elk's mouth looks like. I have included an illustration showing these features. (Refer to Illustration 3.1 in Appendix B.)*

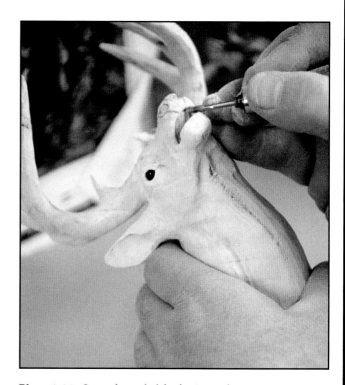

Photo 3.20 *Carve the roof of the deer's mouth.*

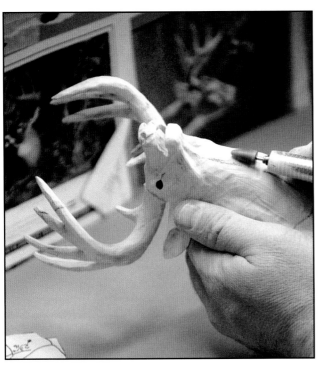

Photo 3.21 *Go over the entire surface of the deer's body, head and antlers with a very fine cone-shaped diamond bit. Smooth everything down as smooth as possible to prepare it for the final details.*

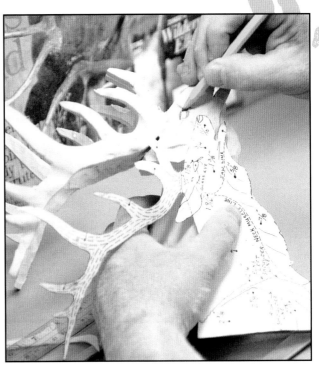

Photo 3.22 *If you are working on a bull elk, mark the eye using the pattern as a guide.*

Photo 3.23 *Mark the neck and shoulders.*

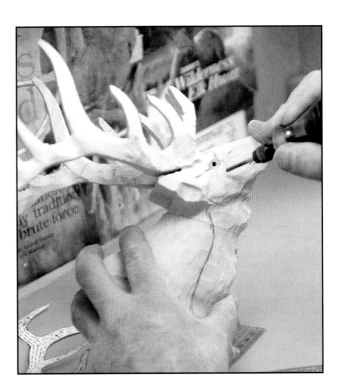

Photo 3.24 *Then drill the permanent eye marking with the drill bit. Remember to only go half way on both sides. If you try to drill all the way through from one side it is very easy to be off center when you come out the other side. It is much easier to measure back from the tip of the nose and down from the top of the forehead, marking the eyes on both sides.*

Photo 3.25 *Return to the antlers to carve off the final remaining bulk.*

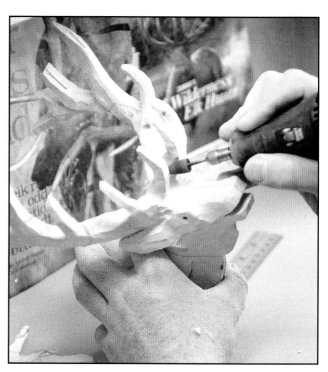

Photo 3.26 *Remember that what ever you trim off of one side or point you then must go to the opposite side or point and trim off the same amount. This will keep both sides even.*

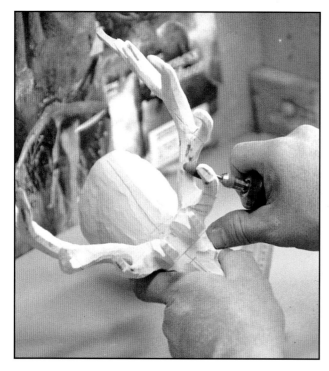

Photo 3.27 *I usually try to take everything off of the main beams on the elk antlers first and leave the points for last. They are a lot narrower and more fragile.*

Photo 3.28 *Start to carve down the larger points, working your way to the smaller ones last.*

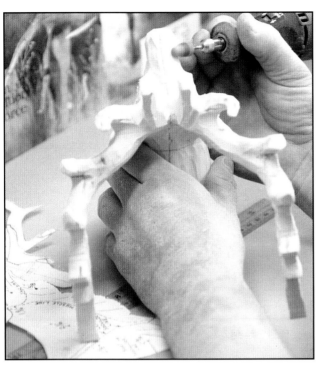

Photo 3.29 *Here I am working down the sides of the elk's head to help bring it into proportion to the front brow points.*

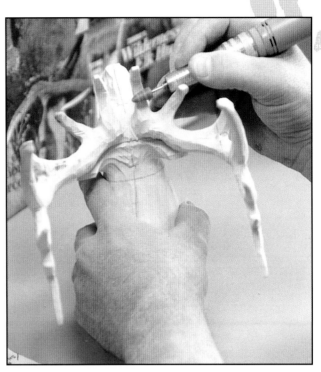

Photo 3.30 *After you have worked down the small points, go over all the points taking out all the rough lines and carved marks in them. I use a fine grit diamond bit for this.*

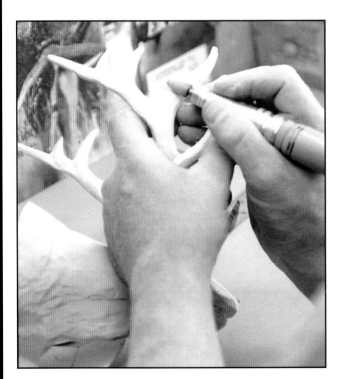

Photo 3.31 *When working the last three or four points on the main beam, sometimes it helps to support the antler with a hand or fingers on the opposite side. This keeps the antler from vibrating and possibly breaking.*

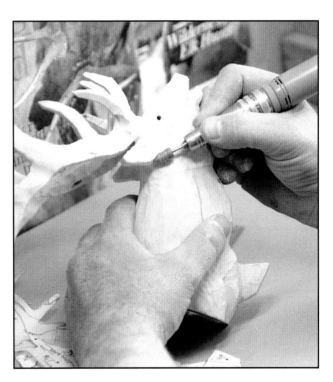

Photo 3.32 *Once the antlers are pretty much carved down to where you want them, begin to shape the front of the ear using a medium grit bit. Then go ahead and remove all the excess wood from behind the ear just as you did with the deer bust.*

Photo 3.33 *At this point you are ready to open up the eye hole with a ball-shaped bit. Remember to open it up around the drilled hole evenly on all sides. I use a 7 mm. dark brown eye for this pattern as we did in the deer head bust. Once you have the hole opened up and have fitted the 7 mm. eye, fill the eye hole with wood filler and press in the eyes on both sides evenly.*

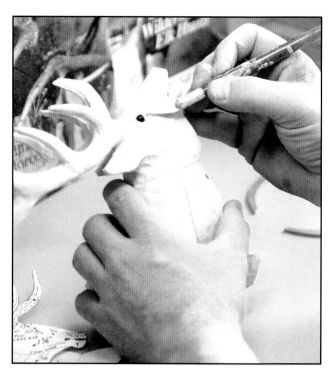

Photo 3.34 *When the filler has had 24 hours to dry, remove the excess dried wood filler from the surface of the eyes. After removing the excess filler if you notice any holes or air bubbles simply fill the holes or bubbles with more filler and allow it to dry again.*

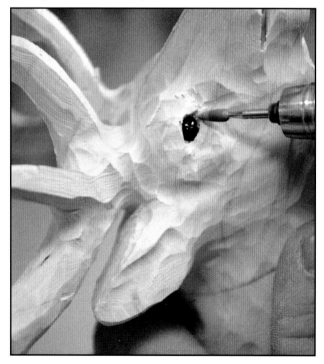

Photo 3.35 *Form the scent gland in front of the bull elk's eye first before you put in the eye lids. I do this by using a small pointed diamond bit.*

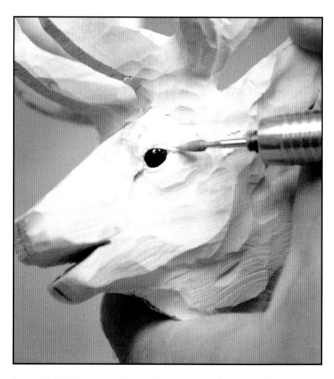

Photo 3.36 *Draw on the eye lids and carve them using the same pointed diamond bit.*

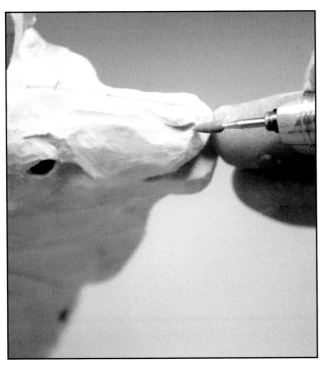

Photo 3.37 *Next cut the nostrils using the same small pointed diamond bit.*

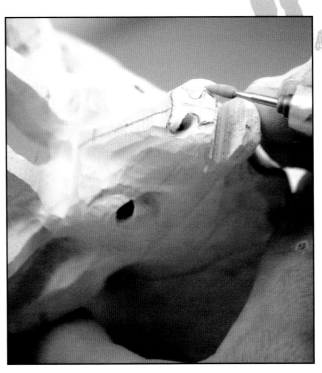

Photo 3.38 *Sometimes it really helps to draw the nose on before carving it down. This helps to keep it even on both sides. Also notice how the center line is still on the elk's forehead and nose. Remember to always leave your center line on until the very last thing. You will always be taking your measurements from it.*

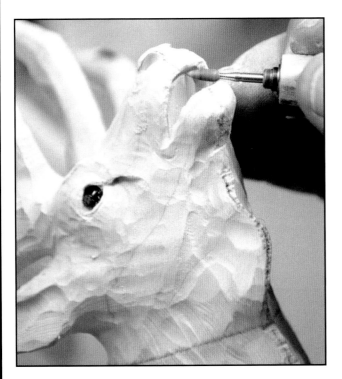

Photo 3.39 *When you complete the nose, you can now start to cut the inside of the mouth. I usually do all the mouth carving using a small pointed bit and a very small round ball-shaped burr.*

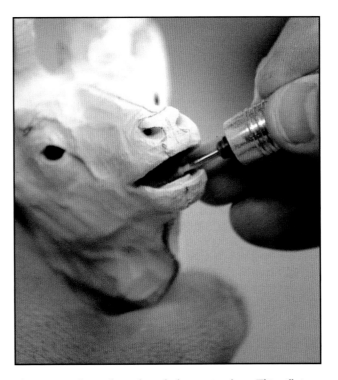

Photo 3.40 *Carve the teeth on the bottom jaw first. This will give me a marker as to where to place the tongue. (Refer to Illustration 3.1 in Appendix B. This has a diagram of the roof of a bull elk's mouth.) The inside of the bottom jaw is the same eys a deer.*

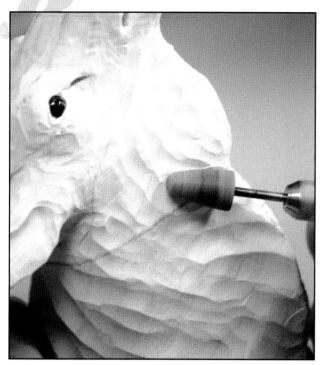

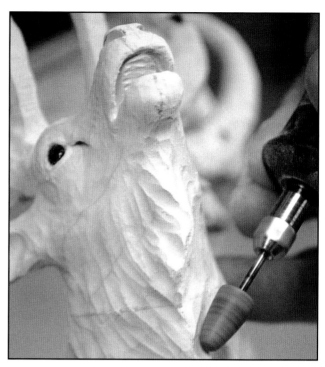

Photo 3.41 *Because the hair on a bull elk's neck is much more coarse and longer than the rest of the body you'll want to prepare the neck for hair by carving large wavy grooves in the neck that run from the bottom it the jaw back to the shoulders. Use a wide coarse cone-shaped diamond bit for this step.*

Photo 3.42 *Bring the carved grooves down to a point on the bottom side of the neck. Now you are ready to prepare the elk for hair texture and antler veining.*

Chapter Four

Hair Texture, Antler Veining and Final Touches

The first point that I would like to make on hair textures and antler veining is that no two animals are alike. Every deer or elk has its own unique way that hair grows and its own unique way that veins form in the antlers. I usually have a lot of fun putting hair on an animal. Bull elks for example have some of the most interesting hair patterns I've carved. There may be one or more different cowlicks on the sides and tops of their heads, or they might not have any. I have included an illustration of both a deer and a bull elk that have basic hair pattern lines drawn on them. These are very basic hair patterns, but it gives a carver a place to start. Refer to Illustrations 4.1 and 4.2 in Appendix B. As far as the veins in the antlers are concerned I will first explain how and where the vein lines come from. This will help you understand the vein process.

When a deer or an elk begins to grow antlers in the spring, blood veins form around the bony structures to provide nutrients as they grow larger throughout the summer. As the antlers grow larger, so do the veins. When the antlers are in the velvet stage, the veins protrude from the outer surface of the antler. As fall approaches and the antlers start to harden, the veins on the outer surface of the antlers dry up and leave a negative groove where the veins once protruded. To prepare the antlers for veining I first begin by drawing on the vein lines with a pencil, as shown in Photo 4.1.

Photo 4.1 *Draw the vein lines on the deer's antler.*

Photo 4.2 *Use a long pointed very coarse diamond bit to cut the vein lines. This will help you get an even cut as you cross the grain of the wood in the antlers.*

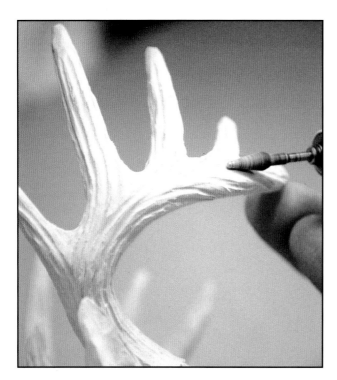

Photo 4.3 *It may be necessary to go over these lines with a fine grit bit to smooth some of the rough edges left by the coarse bit. Remember it also helps to support the antler while working on it with a finger or hand.*

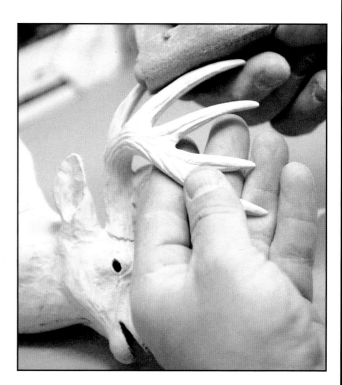

Photo 4.4 *Once the veins are cut on the antlers, use a piece of flexible Swiss sand paper with about 120 grit to sand down the antler tips very smooth. Then sand over the entire surface of the antler.*

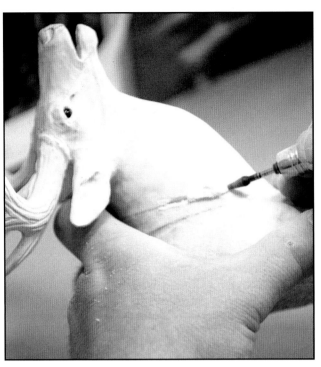

Photo 4.5 *Go back to the splice we made when we first started. Grind a groove approximately $1/8$ of an inch deep right on the seam. Make sure you clean the epoxy or glue out of the groove you just cut.*

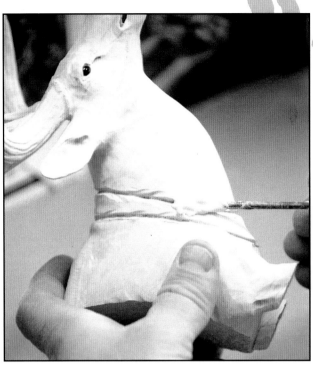

Photo 4.6 *Once the grooves have been cut and cleaned, use wood filler to fill the groove. Allow this to dry 24 hours. I learned this technique from some professional duck carvers. This also works well if you ever have a woodcarving that gets broken or damaged.*

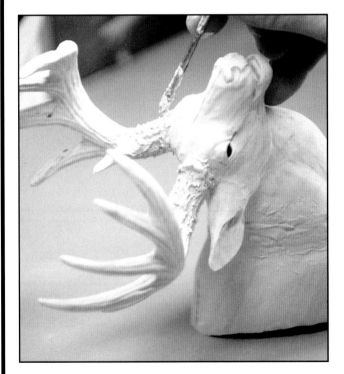

Photo 4.7 *The fast way to duplicate the sharp points on the lower portions of the antlers is to dab wood filler on the antlers, as I have shown here. A better, but more difficult, way is to leave the edges between the veins a little "high." Then take a small cone-shaped stone with a dull point and go in a circular motion over the top of these ridges.*

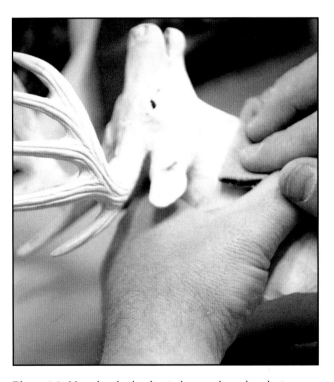

Photo 4.8 *Now that the detailing is done on the antlers, begin preparing the surface of the deer's head, neck, and shoulders for the hair texture. First, sand off the excess wood filler at the joint area and then sand the entire surface smooth.*

Photo 4.9 *When the surface of the deer's body is smooth, go back to the antlers and apply a heavy layer of one ton super glue to the antlers only. When this dries it will make the antlers very strong. You must have all the necessary detail in the antlers before you use the glue, because when the glue dries the wood will be almost impossible to carve.*

Photo 4.10 *Now draw the hair lines on the entire deer's body. This makes the process of putting the hair on much faster. You will then have an easy-to-follow map already on the deer when you begin cutting in the hair.*

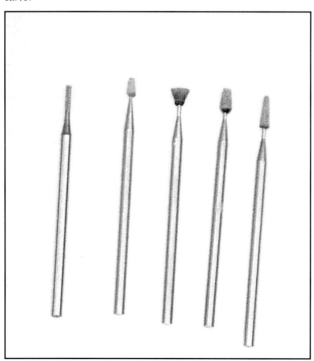

Photo 4.11 *These are some of my favorite hair texturing bits and stones.*

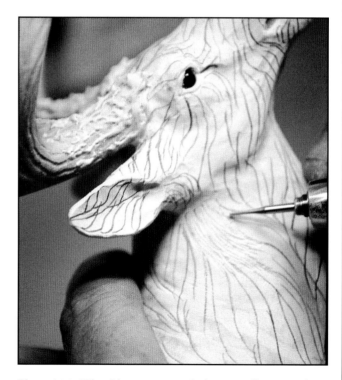

Photo 4.12 *When I begin cutting in the hair I usually start in the hard to get places first, such as behind the ears, between the antlers and around the mouth and eyes.*

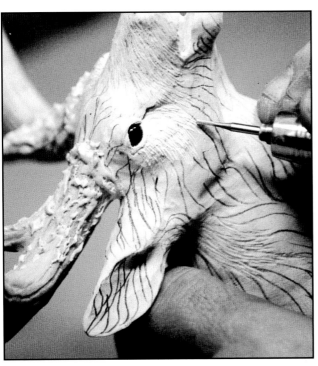

Photo 4.13 *Your hands can tend to sweat, so it is best if you either where a glove or texture the areas that you hold last. The reason for this is that if you texture the areas that you will be holding first, the sweat from your hands will make the hair texture swell in between the harder grains in the wood. This will leave the surface uneven on the finished product.*

Photo 4.14 *When you are cutting hair lines, it is very important to run your bit or stone at a slight angle to the hair lines and "drag" your bit or stone across the surface. This will give you a more natural-looking hair flow.*

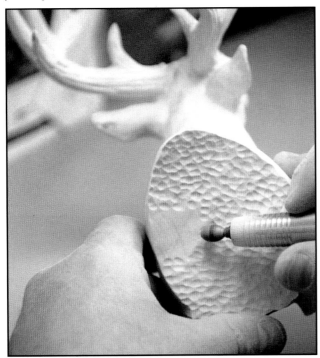

Photo 4.15 *Once the entire deer bust is covered with hair, put a "trademark" texture in the void area on the back of the bust.*

Photo 4.16 *Then prepare the deer for painting by applying a solid coat of clear sanding sealer. This will keep your carving from taking on any moisture. I recommend that a carver never skip this step. This is a very important step to ensure that your carving will last a lifetime.*

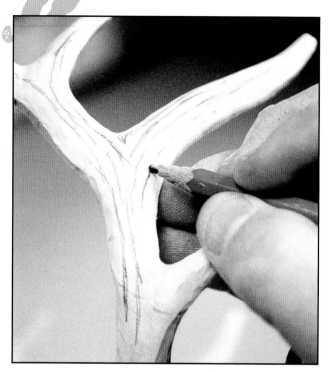

Photo 4.17 *If you're working on a bull elk, begin preparing the elk's antlers for veining by drawing on the vein lines.*

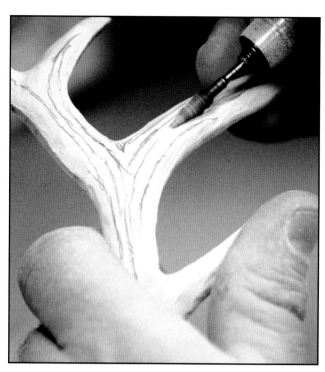

Photo 4.18 *Be careful when cutting the vein lines that you do not to cut them very deep. Approximately 1/32 of an inch is more than enough. After you have the vein put on the antler, sand down the antlers as done with the deer bust.*

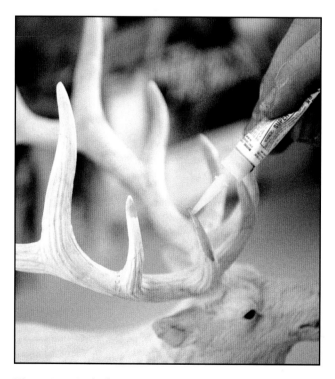

Photo 4.19 *Apply the one ton super glue to strengthen the bull elk's antlers.*

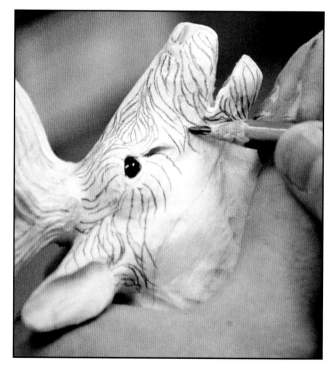

Photo 4.20 *Once the super glue has dried, begin by drawing the hair lines on the elk's body.*

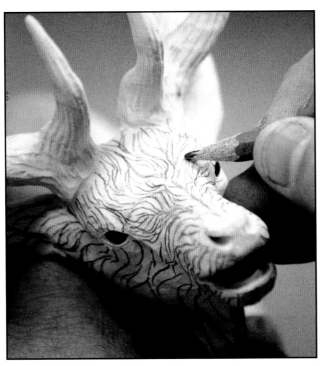

Photo 4.21 *Draw the hair lines on the bull elk's forehead.*

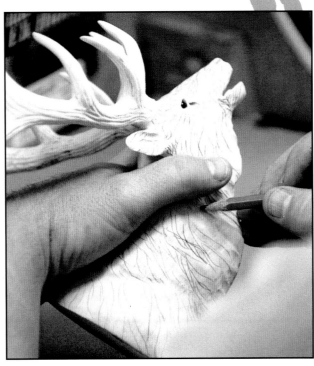

Photo 4.22 *Apply hair lines to the elk's neck and shoulders.*

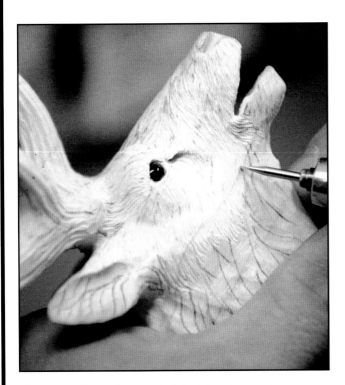

Photo 4.23 *Remember to work the hair lines in an angle.*

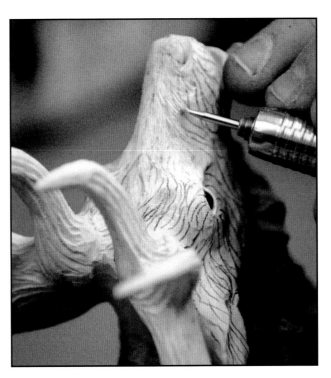

Photo 4.24 *When you cut the hair lines on the elk's head, try to keep the cut very light.*

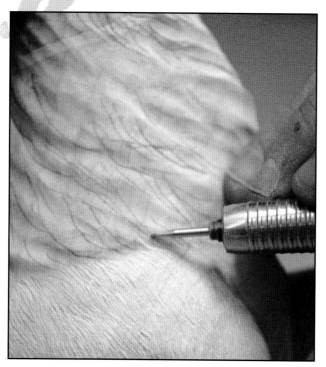

Photo 4.25 *When texturing a bull elk's neck I press the stone a little bit harder than on the head or shoulders. This gives the elk's neck a rougher look in appearance.*

Photo 4.26 *Finish the hair texture on the bull elk's head.*

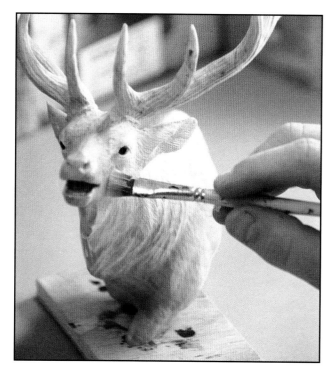

Photo 4.27 *Once the hair texturing is complete, finish by preparing the elk bust for painting by covering it with a coat of clear sanding sealer.*

Chapter Five

Painting Techniques

When I paint a woodcarving, I prefer to use acrylic paints instead of oils. Acrylics tend to give fur and feathers a natural, flat look; oils tend to leave the surface with a slightly satin appearance. When selecting brushes, I like to use very soft brushes that have bristles or hairs no longer than $1/2$ inch in length. I will use about three different brushes for painting a deer or elk bust. The first brush is approximately $1/2$ inch wide by $1/2$ inch long. I use this brush for the light washes that will be applied. The second brush I use is about $1/4$ inch wide and $3/8$ inch long. I use this brush to blend colors around the eye and nose patches, and any other small hard to get to places with the larger brush. The last brush is a very small, fine-tipped brush for the eyes, nose, mouth and other small details.

MULE DEER COLOR
CHART

RAW
SIENA

STEP: 1
BLACK GESSO

STEP: 2
RAW UMBER

STEP: 3
UNBLEACHED
TITANIUM
(WASH)

STEP: 4
RAW SIENA
(WASH)

STEP: 5
RAW UMBER
(WASH)

UNBLEACHED
TITANIUM

MARS BLACK

UNBLEACHED
TITANIUM

MARS
BLACK

UNBLEACHED
TITANIUM

1

2

3

4

5

WHITETAIL DEER COLOR CHART

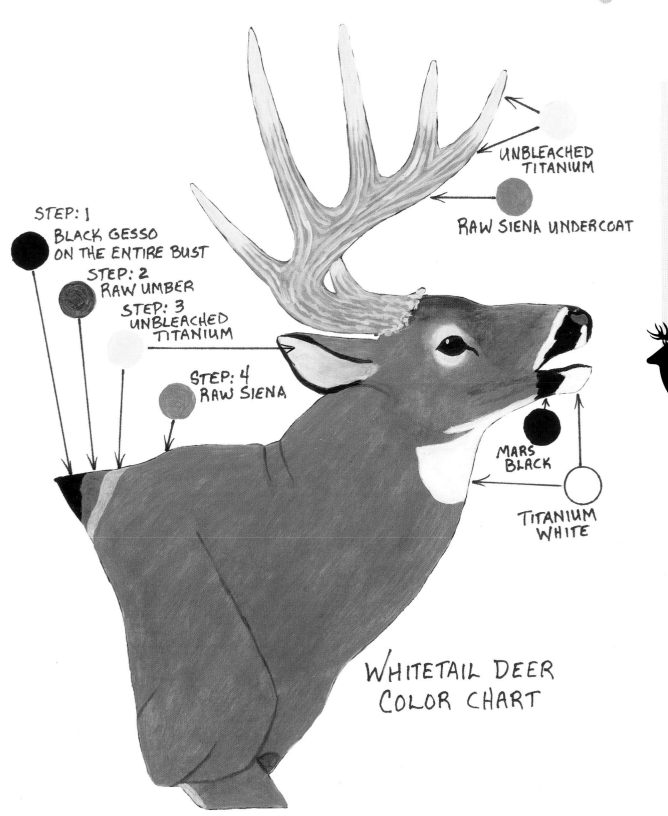

UNBLEACHED TITANIUM

RAW SIENA UNDERCOAT

STEP: 1
BLACK GESSO
ON THE ENTIRE BUST

STEP: 2
RAW UMBER

STEP: 3
UNBLEACHED
TITANIUM

STEP: 4
RAW SIENA

MARS
BLACK

TITANIUM
WHITE

WHITETAIL DEER
COLOR CHART

BULL ELK BUST COLOR
CHART

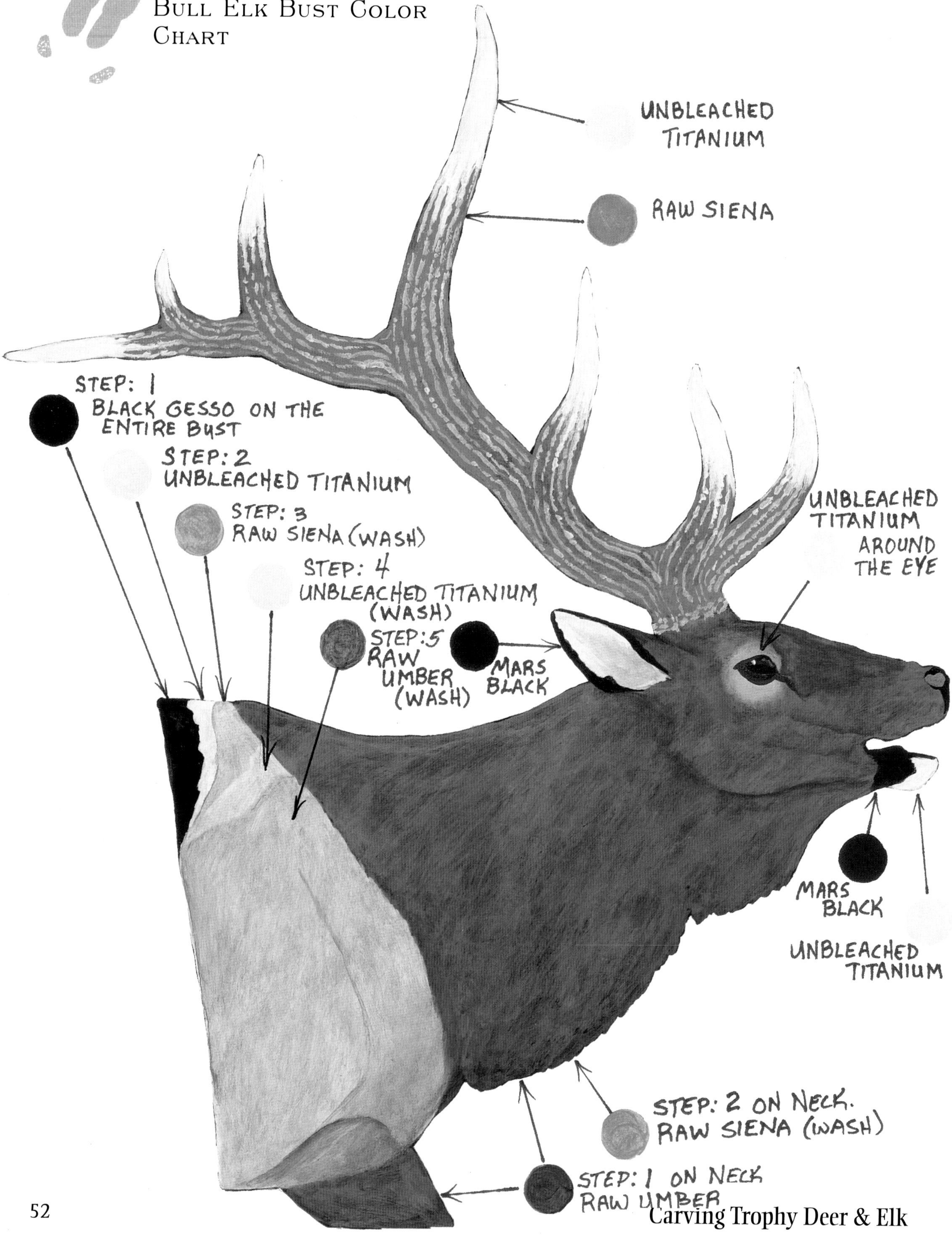

UNBLEACHED
TITANIUM

RAW SIENA

STEP: 1
BLACK GESSO ON THE
ENTIRE BUST

STEP: 2
UNBLEACHED TITANIUM

STEP: 3
RAW SIENA (WASH)

STEP: 4
UNBLEACHED TITANIUM
(WASH)

STEP: 5
RAW
UMBER
(WASH)

MARS
BLACK

UNBLEACHED
TITANIUM
AROUND
THE EYE

MARS
BLACK

UNBLEACHED
TITANIUM

STEP: 2 ON NECK.
RAW SIENA (WASH)

STEP: 1 ON NECK
RAW UMBER

52

Carving Trophy Deer & Elk

Photo 5.1 *Before I start applying any color I always begin with a coat of acrylic primer. I prefer using a black gesso. The reason I use black over other colors is that after you have painted your bust and you accidentally missed a spot on the fur, a deep hair line for example, it simply looks like a dark hair. If you were to use white gesso, the same missed spot would show up like a sore thumb.*

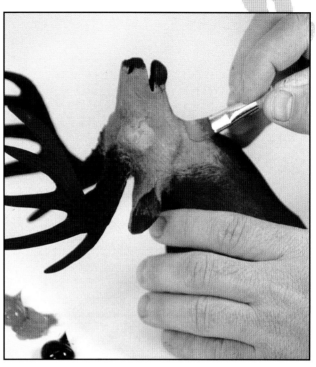

Photo 5.2 *When I begin applying color, I usually start on the head. However, it doesn't really matter where you begin. I start by using three basic colors: unbleached titanium, raw sienna and raw umber. I start with raw umber and add a little of the other two as I apply the umber. Exact tone of brown is not important at this stage, you are just trying to get a first coat of coverage.*

Photo 5.3 *This is the white tail deer bust after the first coat has been applied. Notice how I also have made a lighter halo of unbleached titanium around the eye.*

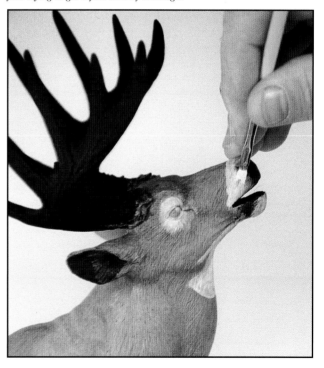

Photo 5.4 *At this point I will also apply the first coat of unbleached titanium on the white tail's nose and light throat patch.*

Photo 5.5 *I also apply unbleached titanium as a first coat on the inner ears.*

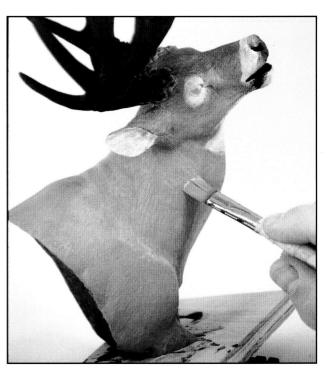

Photo 5.6 *At this point, I believe the white tail is too dark in color, so I will apply a very light wash of raw sienna. This will lighten it up a bit. If I thought the deer was too light, I could add a light wash of raw umber. That is why you shouldn't get too disappointed if you are not pleased with the color of the first coat. It can always be changed.*

Photo 5.7 *I still believe my deer is too dark, so I add another light wash of raw sienna mixed 50/50 with unbleached titanium. There is no limit on the number of washes that can be applied. You can just keep applying them until you achieve the color you like.*

Photo 5.8 *Now that I have the color that I want for the body, I apply the first coat on the antlers. This is strictly raw sienna.*

Photo 5.9 *I have now begun adding the black facial markings of a white tail buck. It may be necessary to apply another coat of unbleached titanium to the throat patch and nose before you apply the black facial markings, especially, if you didn't get a heavy enough coverage earlier.*

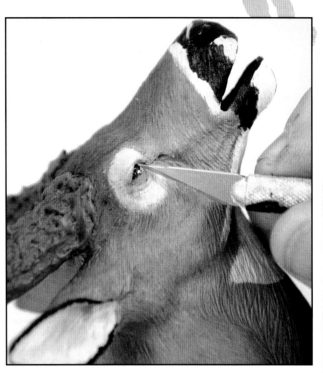

Photo 5.10 *Before I paint the black eyelids I first clean the paint off of the glass eye using an exacto-knife.*

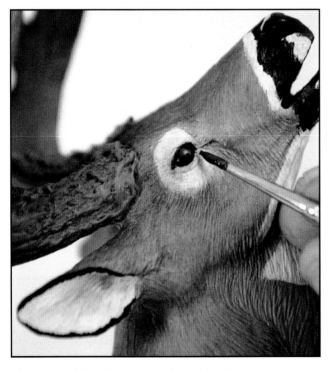

Photo 5.11 *I then begin painting the eyelids with a small, fine, soft brush.*

Photo 5.12 *Now I apply the second layer of color to the antlers. This is raw umber.*

Photo 5.13 *When the antlers are dry, begin "wisping" unbleached titanium on the antlers using the largest brush. To do this, fill your brush full of paint and then wipe the paint out of your brush with a cloth rag. There will still be paint in the brush. Now just wipe or wisp the brush back and forth over the antlers. This will put unbleached titanium on all of the high spots of the antlers. This is what makes the veining show up.*

Photo 5.14 *Be careful not to get too much paint on your brush or this high lighting technique will not work.*

Photo 5.15 *This "wisping" technique may need to be done two or three times to achieve the color of the antlers that suits you.*

Photo 5.16 *All that is left are the final touches. Here I paint the nose black. I have also painted the inside of the nose and mouth pink.*

Photo 5.17 *I paint the front teeth with unbleached titanium.*

Photo 5.18 *I finish by painting the nose inside and out with a clear high gloss finish. The very last thing I do is mount the deer to a small wood base, usually oak or walnut, by running a screw up through the bottom into the deer's leg.*

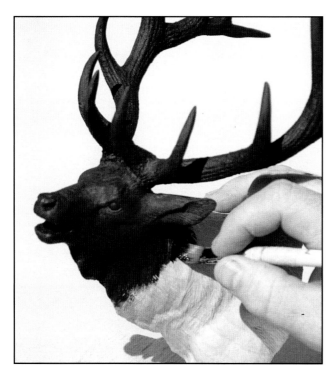

Photo 5.19 *If you're working on an elk, begin by painting the elk bust with black gesso.*

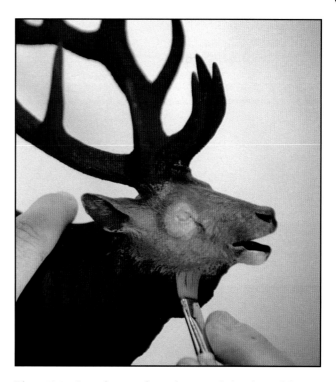

Photo 5.20 *I use the same three colors as with the white tail deer: raw sienna, unbleached titanium and raw umber. Bull elk are a lot darker on their head and neck than most deer, so I go heavy on the raw umber at this stage of applying the first coat.*

Photo 5.21 *An elk has a very light-colored body, so I start with unbleached titanium with just a little raw umber for the first layer on the bull's shoulders.*

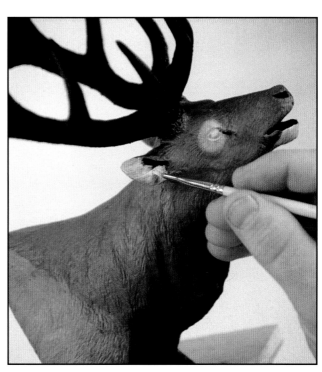

Photo 5.22 *Apply the light ear and chin markings using unbleached titanium.*

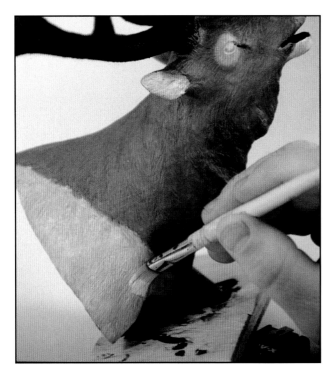

Photo 5.23 *At this point, I think the shoulders are too dark, so I apply a light wash of unbleached titanium to lighten them up.*

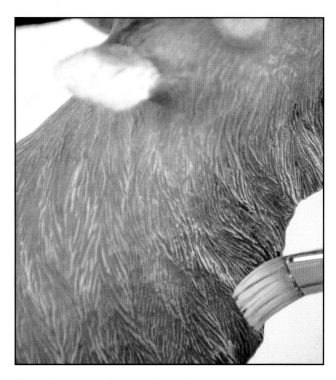

Photo 5.24 *I now "wisp" unbleached titanium on the neck to highlight hair and give it depth. Do this very lightly so you only get the light colorations on the high areas.*

Photo 5.25 *At this point I begin applying the first layer on the antlers. I use raw sienna on the lower beams and points. Then come down from the top of the points with unbleached titanium.*

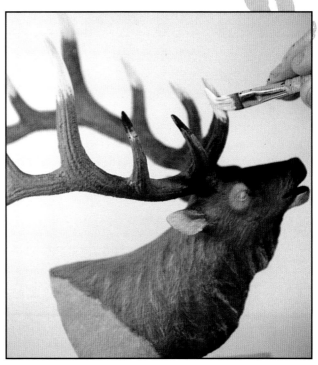

Photo 5.26 *Be careful not to bring the unbleached titanium antler tips down very far on the points.*

Photo 5.27 *While I am waiting for the antler to dry, I move on to all of the small details. I can paint the nose, chin patch, eye lids and the edges around the ears black. I also paint the inside of the elk's mouth and nose a purplish pink.*

Photo 5.28 *I can now apply the second layer on the bull elk's antlers by using plain raw umber. I apply this only to the lower portions on which I applied the raw sienna earlier.*

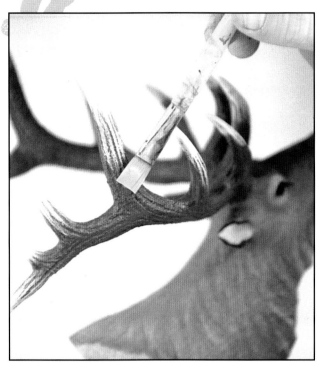

Photo **5.29** *I now lightly "wisp" a light layer of unbleached titanium starting at the antler tips and working your way down.*

Photo **5.30** *Go lighter as you go down the antler points. You are only trying to add very light highlights to the lower elk antler beams.*

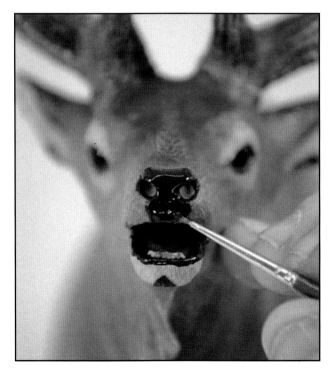

Photo **5.31** *I finish off the elk bust by painting the bull's teeth with unbleached titanium and applying a clear high gloss finish to the elk's nose and mouth. This makes his nose and mouth look wet. This also gives him added life.*

Photo **5.32** *The bull elk bust is now ready to mount to a wood base.*

Photo 5.33 *If you're working on a mule deer, paint the entire buck painted with black gesso.*

Photo 5.34 *I use the same three colors as with the white tail deer and elk bust: unbleached titanium, raw sienna and raw umber. This is a mule deer after the first coat has been applied. A mule deer has a much lighter face than a white tail deer, so I have gone heavy on the unbleached titanium around the mule deer's face.*

Photo 5.35 *I have added a light wash of raw sienna mixed 50/50 with unbleached titanium to lighten the mule deer.*

Photo 5.36 *I then add the dark forehead markings with a light wash of mars black mixed 50/50 with raw umber.*

Photo 5.37 *Here I added a darkened nose patch using raw umber.*

Photo 5.38 *I then add all of the many fine details at this point by painting the inner ears with unbleached titanium and a black lining around the ears. Then blacken in the nose, nose markings and eye lids.*

Photo 5.39 *On the antlers of a mule deer buck I use the three simple stages used on the white tail's and elk's antlers. Start with raw sienna, allow to dry. Then apply raw umber over the antlers and allow to dry. Then "wisp" unbleached titanium until you achieve the desired coloration. Your mule deer is now ready to mount on a wooden base.*

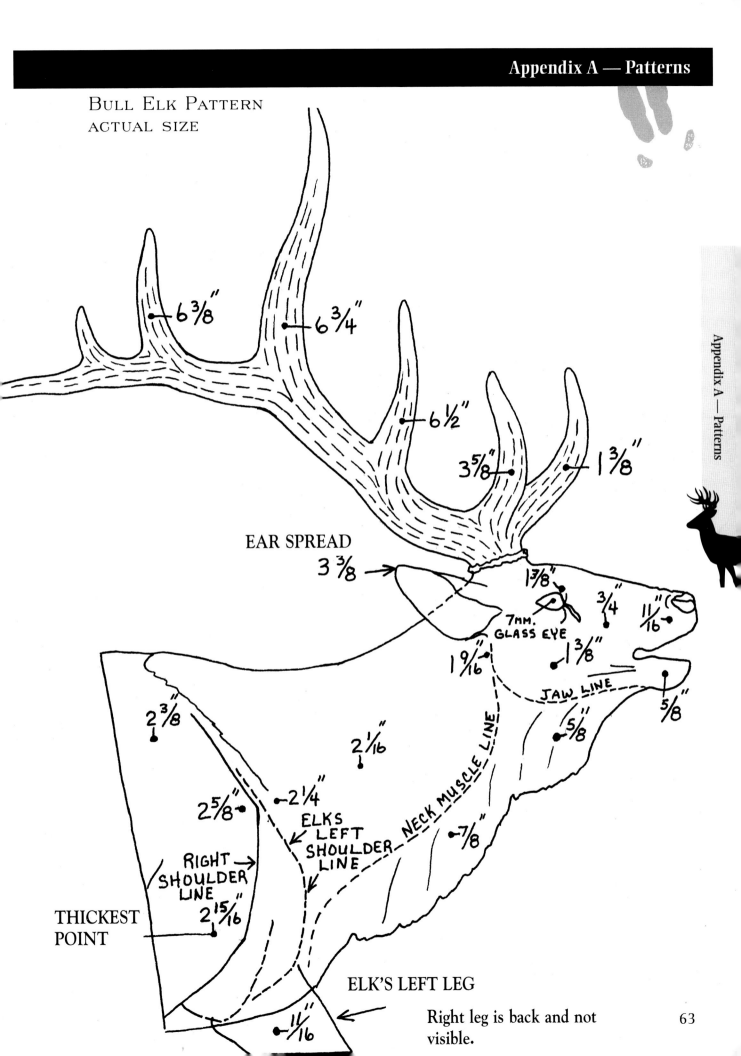

BULL ELK PATTERN
ACTUAL SIZE

6 3/8"

6 3/4"

6 1/2"

3 5/8"

1 3/8"

EAR SPREAD
3 3/8

1 3/8"

3/4"

1 1/16"

7MM.
GLASS EYE

1 9/16"

1 3/8"

JAW LINE

5/8"

2 3/8"

2 1/16"

5/8"

2 5/8"

2 1/4"

ELKS
LEFT
SHOULDER
LINE

NECK MUSCLE LINE

7/8"

RIGHT
SHOULDER
LINE

THICKEST
POINT

2 15/16"

ELK'S LEFT LEG

1 1/16"

Right leg is back and not
visible.

BULL ELK PATTERN—TOP VIEW

ACTUAL SIZE

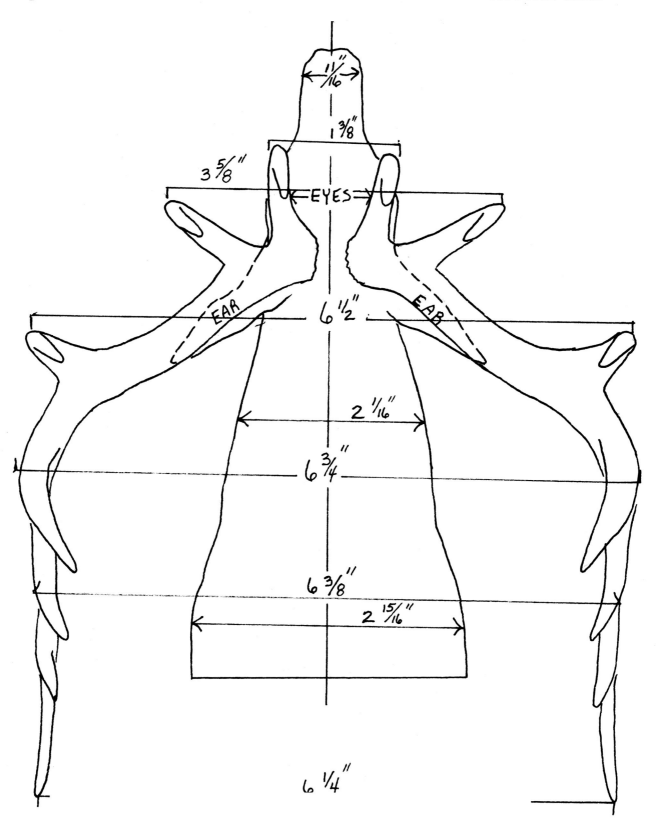

Carving Trophy Deer & Elk

WHITETAIL BUCK PATTERN

ACTUAL SIZE

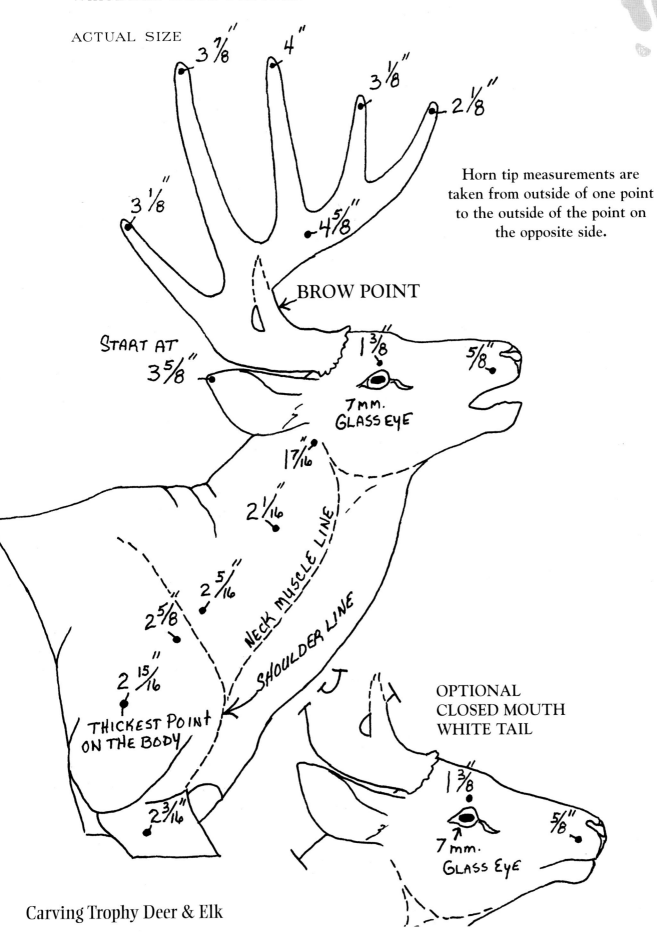

3 7/8"

4"

3 1/8"

2 1/8"

3 1/8"

Horn tip measurements are taken from outside of one point to the outside of the point on the opposite side.

4 5/8"

BROW POINT

START AT 3 5/8"

1 3/8"

5/8"

7 MM. GLASS EYE

1 7/16"

2 1/16"

Neck muscle line

SHOULDER LINE

2 5/16"

2 5/8"

2 15/16"

THICKEST POINT ON THE BODY

2 3/16"

OPTIONAL CLOSED MOUTH WHITE TAIL

1 3/8"

5/8"

7 MM. GLASS EYE

Carving Trophy Deer & Elk

Whitetail Buck Pattern—Top View

Actual Size

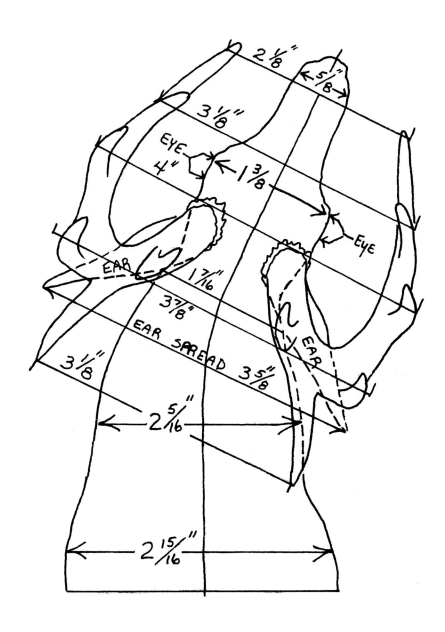

2 ⅛"

⅝"

3 ⅛"

EYE
4"

1 ⅜"

EYE

EAR

1 ⁷⁄₁₆"

3 ⅞"

EAR

EAR SPREAD 3 ⅝"

3 ⅛"

2 ⁵⁄₁₆"

2 ¹⁵⁄₁₆"

MULE DEER PATTERN

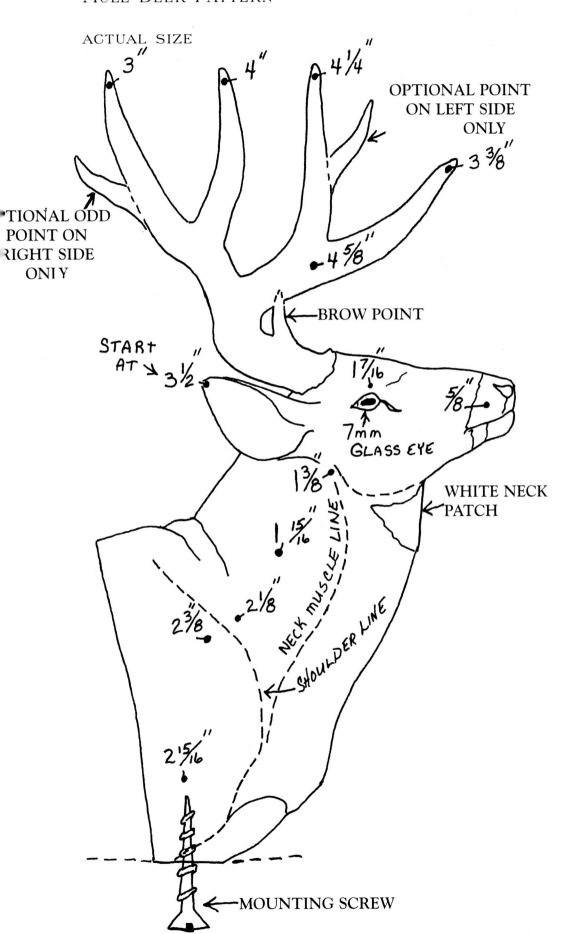

ACTUAL SIZE

3"

4"

4¼"

OPTIONAL POINT
ON LEFT SIDE
ONLY

3 ⅜"

OPTIONAL ODD
POINT ON
RIGHT SIDE
ONLY

4 ⅝"

BROW POINT

START
AT → 3½"

1 ⁷⁄₁₆"

5⁄8"

7mm
GLASS EYE

WHITE NECK
PATCH

1⅜"

1 ¹⁵⁄₁₆"

NECK MUSCLE LINE

2⅛"

2⅜"

SHOULDER LINE

2 ¹⁵⁄₁₆"

MOUNTING SCREW

MULE DEER PATTERN—TOP VIEW

ACTUAL SIZE

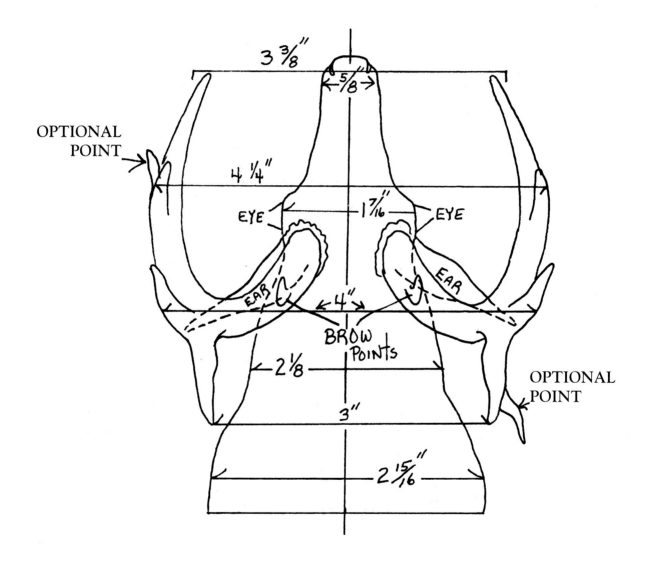

OPTIONAL
POINT

OPTIONAL
POINT

3 3/8"

5/8

4 1/4"

EYE   1 7/16"   EYE

EAR   EAR

4"

BROW
POINTS

2 1/8

3"

2 15/16"

Illus. 1.1 — Bull Elk Skeletal System

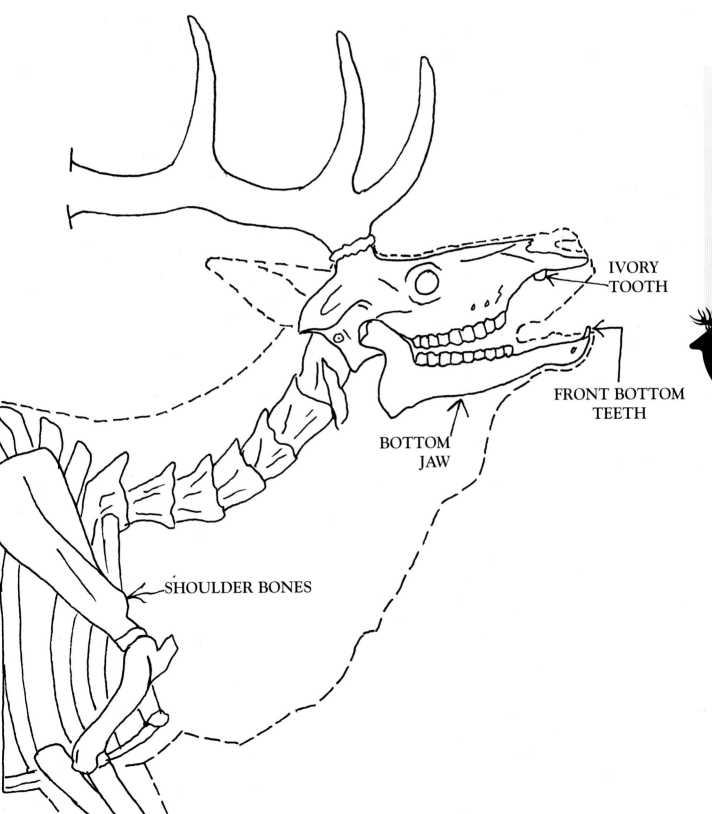

IVORY TOOTH

FRONT BOTTOM TEETH

BOTTOM JAW

SHOULDER BONES

ILLUS. 3.1 — INSIDE OF A DEER'S MOUTH

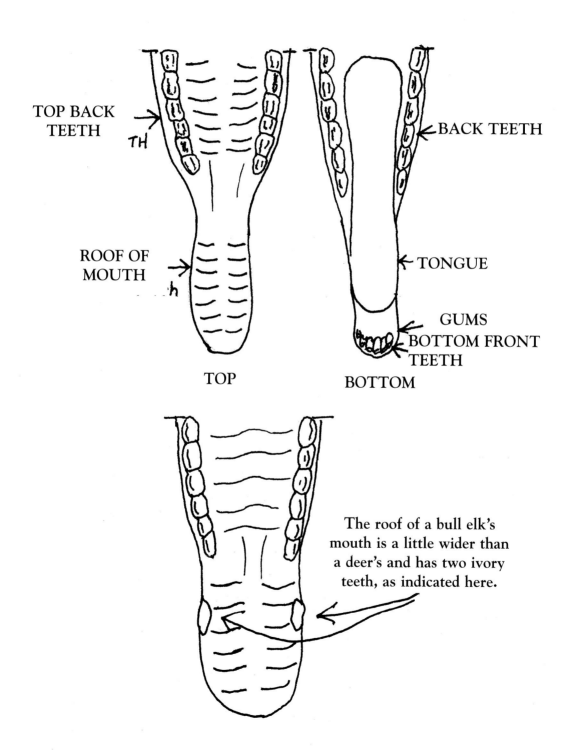

TOP BACK TEETH

TH

ROOF OF MOUTH

h

TOP

BACK TEETH

TONGUE

GUMS
BOTTOM FRONT TEETH

BOTTOM

The roof of a bull elk's mouth is a little wider than a deer's and has two ivory teeth, as indicated here.

Illus. 3.2 — Antler Veining

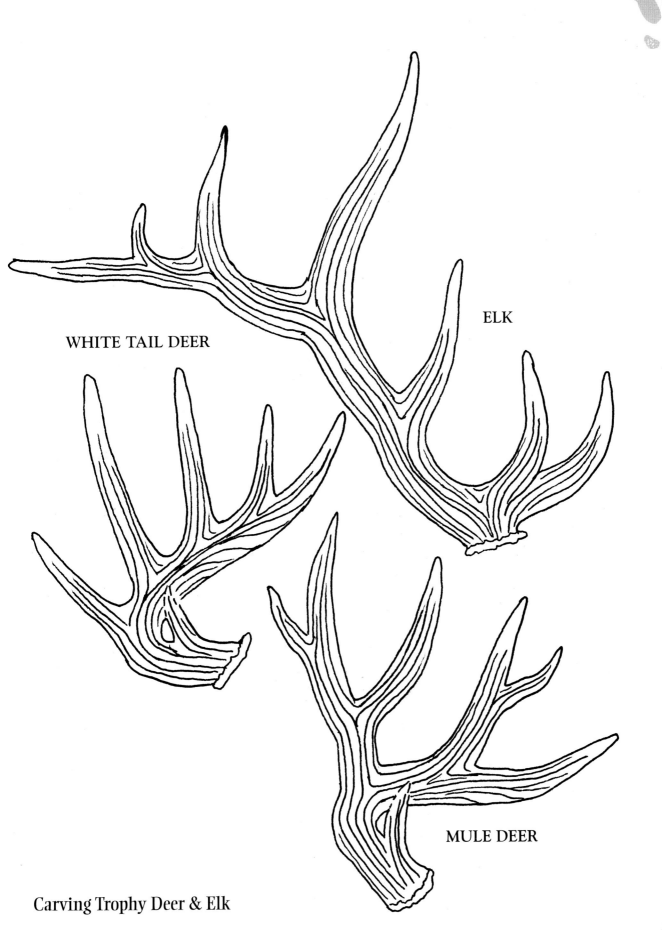

WHITE TAIL DEER

ELK

MULE DEER

Carving Trophy Deer & Elk

ILLUS. 4.1 — DIRECTION HAIR FLOW PATTERNS

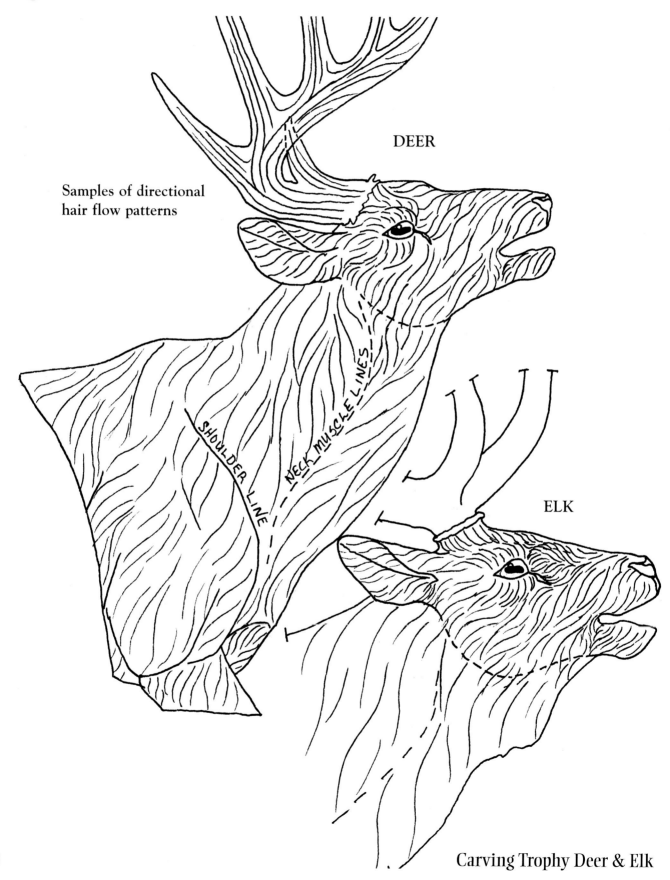

DEER

Samples of directional
hair flow patterns

SHOULDER LINE

NECK MUSCLE LINES

ELK

Carving Trophy Deer & Elk

ILLUS. 4.2 — DIRECTIONAL HAIR FLOW PATTERNS

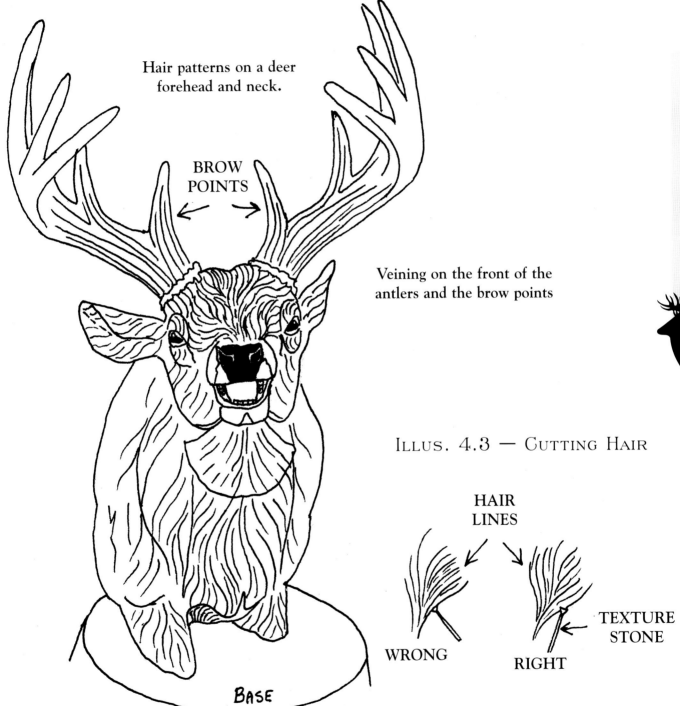

Hair patterns on a deer forehead and neck.

BROW POINTS

Veining on the front of the antlers and the brow points

BASE

ILLUS. 4.3 — CUTTING HAIR

HAIR LINES

WRONG

RIGHT

TEXTURE STONE

When cutting hair with a small stone with an edge, drag it across the hair lines, not in line with the hair lines.

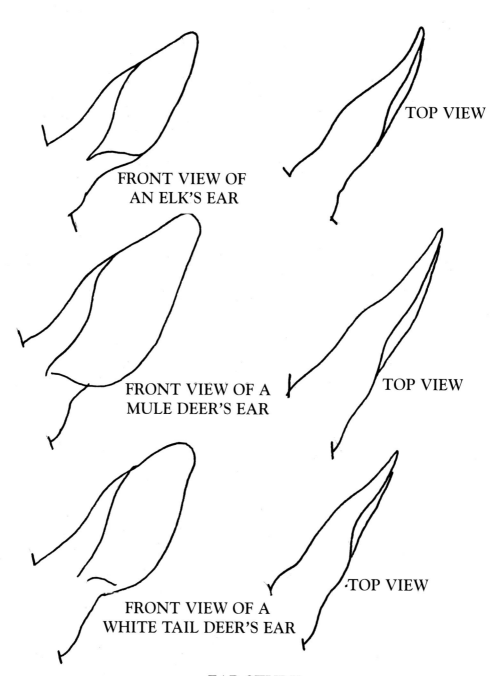

FRONT VIEW OF
AN ELK'S EAR

TOP VIEW

FRONT VIEW OF A
MULE DEER'S EAR

TOP VIEW

FRONT VIEW OF A
WHITE TAIL DEER'S EAR

·TOP VIEW

EAR STUDY
Shows shape only, not comparable sizes.

FOX BOOKS Fox Chapel Publishing Co. Inc.

Learn Carving from These Experts!

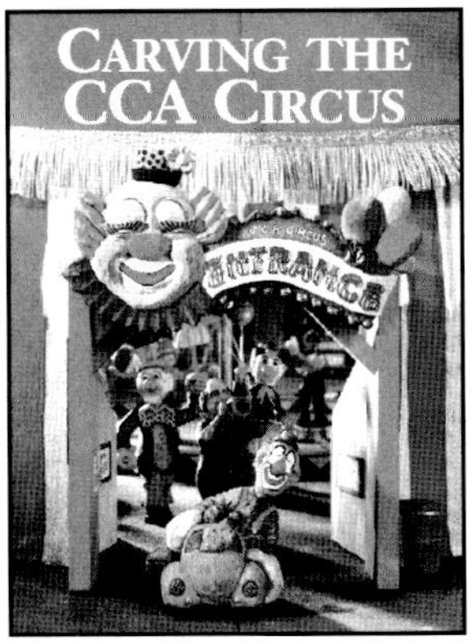

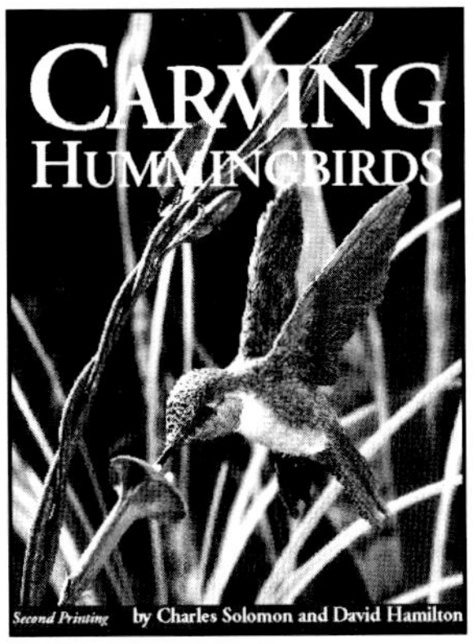

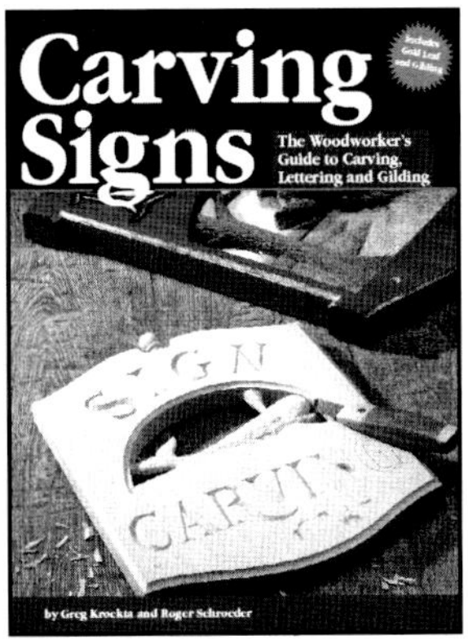

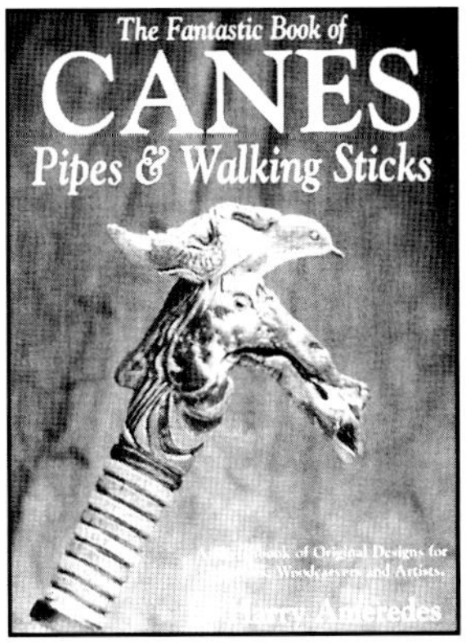

Caricature Carvers of America (CCA)

Carving The CCA Circus NEW!
Here in the pages of this book, you'll get an insider's look at the CCA's latest and most ambitious project to date–the CCA Circus. Enjoy the creative talent and craftsmanship of 23 of the best–known names in caricature carving. Short essays and carving tips from each carver as they detail the creation of their favorite pieces. Man–eating tigers, bumbling clowns, beautiful acrobats, popcorn vendors... They're all here under the CCA big top.
49 patterns inside. **$19.95**

Carving The Full Moon Saloon
Caricature carvers will delight in the work of this group of great carvers. 21 members including well known teachers like Harold Enlow, Claude Bolton, Steve Prescott, Desiree Hajny, Tom Wolfe and Jack Price. Together, these members created "The Full Moon Saloon" a scale model measuring 4 feet long and containing over 40 carvings. Carving the Full Moon Saloon is a 120 page color guide to the creative work involved in these characters. Close up photos show incredible details. Includes patterns and painting technique section.
softcover **$19.95**
Hardcover limited edition **$29.95**

Mary Duke Guldan Titles

Chip Chats columnist Mary Duke Guldan ("Let's Carve!" Column) patterns are the best, most complete available. They show every angle – top view, side, bottom front and back. Along with the patterns show offers clear easy to follow carving instructions. Highly recommended.

Woodcarver's Workbook Carving Animals with Mary Duke Guldan
Called the "best woodcarving pattern book in 40 years" by NWCA president Ed Gallenstein. Carving instructions and detailed information on 9 realistic projects including dogs, moose, wolves, whitetail deer, wild horses & more.
$14.95

Woodcarver's Workbook #2
All new projects (no repeats from book #1 above). Projects inside: Native Indian Chief, buffalo, elk, horses, mules, cattle and oxen, plus a country farmer pattern. **$14.95**

Complete Beginners Woodcarvers Workbook
Mary brings her talents for teaching and pattern drafting to the challenge of designing good looking projects that can be completed by the beginner with a minimum of tools. Learn both carving in the round and relief carving in this book of 10 projects. Over 200 illustrations. **$9.95**

Desiree Hajny Titles

Big Cats by Desiree Hajny
Carving Lions, Tigers and Jaguars. Desi's new full color guide to carving these majestic predators. 100's of color photos and anatomy charts guide you through creating your own masterpiece. Also features painting instructions and reference photos of live animals. **$14.95**

Mammals: An Artistic Approach by Desiree Hajny (second printing)
Carvers will learn to carve realistic north American mammals– deer, bear and offer in this informative 150 page book. Carving techniques for both hand tool and powercarvers are covered plus much needed info on texturing woodburning and painting. **$19.95**

Carving Caricature Animals by Desiree Hajny
Learn how to make caricature carvings based on real animals. Desi shows you how to use cartooning techniques to emphasize an animal's most recognizable characteristics – and then turn those ideas into a caricature carving. Includes over 100 color photos, step–by–step carving and painting techniques, and patterns. **$14.95**

Carving Small Animals
In this comprehensive book, Desi includes everything you'll need to carve rabbits, raccoons and squirrels. Anatomy sketches, descriptions of the animals, and reference photos give you a detailed look at your subject. Charts and photos outline techniques for carving and painting in a step–by–step fashion. Includes pattern, too! **$14.95**

Character Carving Titles

Carving Blockheads by Steve Prescott
What is a Blockhead? A Blockhead is basic shape roughout that can be carved into infinite character–filled personalities. Join Steve as he carved a basic blockhead and then features patterns and color photos of 50 more Blockheads–doctors, nurses, policeman, gnomes...and many more. An exciting new look at carving! **$12.95**

Cowtown Carving Carving Characters
with Texas Whittling Champion Steve Prescott
15 projects including Cowtown Santa, Rodeo Clown and lots of cowboys! Steve includes both a full size bandsaw roughout pattern and a detail pattern for each project. Good pattern book for the intermediate and advanced carver.
$14.95

Whittling the Old Sea Captain and Crew by Mike Shipley
An exciting book on caricature style from this Ozarks Mountain carver. Mike makes his living as a full–time carver. Over 100 photos and color painting guide plus patterns. **$12.95**

Carving Scrooge and Dickens Characters
Patterns for carving the characters from Dicken's "A Christmas Carol"
$12.95

Carving Vermont Folk Figures with Power
by Frank Russell, the Author of "Carving Realistic Animals with Power" offers an exciting collection of characters from the Bachelor to The Logger ready to use patterns included. **$9.95**

Jim Maxwell Titles

Ozarks carver Jim Maxwell has been teaching and carving around Branson, MO for over 25 years. Jim's work shows clean lines, smooth finish and original patterns. The step–by–step photos in his Clown and Movie Characters books leave nothing out. Every cut is shown and explained.

Carving Clowns with Jim Maxwell
Over 200 b/w and color photos introduce you to the humorous world of clowns. Complete how to information for carving and painting. Patterns for 12 different clowns included inside. Highly Recommended! **$14.95**

Woodcarving Adventure Movie Characters
An excellent how to carve book using characters from Jim's favorite silver screen heroes as inspiration. Carve a sailor, cowboy or 21 other exciting characters. All patterns included inside. Over 150 step–by–step photos.
$12.95

Carving Characters
12 favorite projects for hillbillies, farmers, soldiers, even a Turkey Buzzard!
$6.95

Making Collectible Santas and Christmas Ornaments
8 creative Santas and 34 ornament patterns. **$6.95**

Bird Carving Titles

Carving Hummingbirds BEST SELLER!
by Chuck Solomon and David Hamilton
Full color guide to carving and painting "hummers". Patterns for broadtail and ruby throat included. 100's of photos in full color. Reference material on anatomy, wings and habitat.
Highly Recommended! **$19.95**

Encyclopedia of Bird Reference Drawings by David Mohardt
Detailed sketches, wing studies and reference info for carvers. 215 different varieties of birds covered. Recommended by Larry Barth, Bob Guge.
$14.95

George Lehman Carving Pattern Books

Minnesota carver George Lehman's pattern books are a very useful source for beginning and intermediate carvers. Tips, sketches and techniques are sprinkled throughout each book. Write or call for a complete listing of patterns available in Series.

Book One: Carving 20 Realistic Game and Songbirds
Partial list: common loon, chickadee, owl, mallard, grouse, robin, pintails.
$19.95

Book Two: Realism in Wood
Partial list: bald eagle, kingfisher, pheasants, bobwhite, great horned owl, pileated woodpecker, red–tailed hawk, mockingbird.
$19.95

Book Three: Nature in Wood
Partial list: barnswallow, cardinal, warblers (3), wrens, goldfinch plus 10 animal patterns. **$16.95**

Other Carving Titles

Carving Signs NEW!
by Roger Schroeder and Greg Krockta
At last a complete manual on carving high quality sign work. Every area is covered in over 250 color photos –choosing wood, carving techniques, laying out and designing the work special tools required, finishing techniques, 12 complete alphabets for signwork plus a pattern treasury of 30 designs are also inside. Learn from professional signcarver, Greg's been in the business for 20 years. **$24.95**

Carving Fish – Miniature Saltwater and Freshwater by Jim Jensen
These detailed patterns, woodburning tips, color painting sections and step–by–step photos show you how to carve 26 different miniature fish for sale or display. **$14.95**

Carousel Horse Carving
An instruction workbook by Ken Hughes. Recommended as a classic how–to–on carving carousel horses. Ken shows you everything step–by–step in making a Denzel style carving in 1/3 standard size. Over 150 photos. New edition includes full size fold out pattern. **$24.95**

Fantastic Book of Canes, Pipes and Walking Sticks by Harry Ameredes
This WV artist and carver had made canes for over 30 years. In these hundred of detailed drawings you'll find lots of ideas for canes, weathered wood and pipes. Plus info on collecting tree roots for carving. **$12.95**

Bark Carving by Joyce Buchanan
Learn carve faces – mystical woodspirits and other expressions in bark. Colorful guide with patterns and lots of helpful info on harvesting bark.
$12.95

Sculpturing Totem Poles by Walt Way
Easy to follow pattern and instruction manual. Lots of clear drawings plus three patterns inside. **$6.95**

Carving Wooden Critters
Diane Ernst carves appealing animals that are best described as realistic caricatures. 16 high quality patterns for rabbits, puppies, otters and more.
$6.95

Realistic Duck Carving (Second Edition) by Alfred Ponte NEW!
At last a simplified easy to follow guide for beginner and intermediate carvers. Tried and true carving method taught by Al to 100's of carvers. Heavily illustrated, color painting charts and reference photos. **$9.95**

Free Form Chip Carving by Carole Ponte
Learn to carve animals, birds and flowers in this easy to learn method. 36 patterns included. **$7.95**

Making Classic Chairs by Ron Clarkson
THE book for classic furniture carving 300+ photos show you gadrooning, decorative relief carving and carving long feet. Includes measured drawings and valuable color gallery. **$24.95**

Tina Toney

Easy Weekend Carving Projects.
A full color guide to carving great small projects, using commercial turnings. Tina's patterns are designed to wrap around wooden eggs for easy transfer. Nice collection of patterns –Santas, animals, old man. . . etc.
$12.95

Santas and Snowmen
Tina's book for Christmas carvings. Beautiful original designs like you've never seen before. 12 patterns and complete step–by–step directions for carving and painting in full color. **$12.95**

Please try your favorite book supplier first!

CREDIT CARD ORDERS MAY CALL

1–800–457–9112

MAIL ORDERS PLEASE SEND BOOK PRICE PLUS **$2.50** PER BOOK (MAXIMUM **$5** SHIPPING CHARGE) TO:

Fox Chapel Publishing
1970 Broad Street
East Petersburg, PA 17520
FAX (717) 560-4702

Wood Carving ILLUSTRATED

Subscribe Today! First Issue October, 1

INSIDE OUR FIRST ISSUE

Harold Enlow: Tribute and Showcase
A special full color tribute with a gallery of his work over the years.

Frank Russell's Power Carving Column

Hand-carving a House Sign

Relief Carving with **David Bennett**

Carve Your Own Custom Name Tag

David Sabol: Santa and Rudolph How-to and Pattern

Desiree Hajny on Painting Techniques

Sharpening: 5 Common Mistakes and How to Avoid Them

Carver's Travel Guide to **Branson,** MO

...plus more!

HAROLD ENLOW • SHARPENING SECRETS • CARVING WOOD SIGNS

Wood Carving ILLUSTRATED
Volume 1, Number 1
$5.95

Woodcarver's Guide to Branson

Chock-full of how-to articles

Every issue 3-hole punched for easy reference

4 big issues each year

Each issue in full color & 64 pages long

Highest quality color and printing

YOU ARE INVITED TO BECOME A CHARTER SUBSCRIBER

Fox Chapel Publishing is pleased to announce North America's new magazine for carvers – covering every type of carving. For a long time we've sensed a need for a general interest how-to carving magazine. After listening to many carvers' suggestions, we've come up with what we think is the perfect answer – **Wood Carving Illustrated Magazine**.

Inside our pages you'll find your favorite type of carving covered in gorgeous full color. From relief carving to Santas, birds, ornaments, wood spirits, caricatures – you name it! Both hand tool and power carving will be included. Our focus is on how-to articles. Lots of "meat" in each issue from North America's top carvers.

You already know many of these folks - Harold Enlow, Roger Schroeder, Frank Russell, Desiree Hajny, David Sabol, David Bennett and Harley Refsal are among the many top carvers featured in **Wood Carving Illustrated**.

If you love woodcarving – you'll love **Wood Carving Illustrated Magazine** – and we'll guarantee it!

Alan Giagnocavo
Publisher

❏ **Yes!** Please enroll me as a Charter Subscriber at the low rate of only $19.95 (a $4 savings).
Start my subscription immediately.
I will get 4 quarterly issues per year. My check or money order for $19.95 is enclosed.
(**You may also subscribe by phone 1-800-457-9112 or fax this form to 717-560-4702.**)

Name: _____

Address: _____

City: _____ State: _____ Zip: _____

Country: _____

Mail to:
Woodcarving Illustrated Magazine
1970 Broad Street
East Petersburg PA 17520

FOX BOOKS
Fox Chapel Publishing Co Inc.

Fox Chapel Publishing
"Publishers of practical books for woodworkers and carvers."